TEACHER'S PET PUBLICATIONS

LITPLAN TEACHER PACK
for
The Midwife's Apprentice
based on the book by
Karen Cushman

Written by
Janine H. Sherman

© 1998 Teacher's Pet Publications
All Rights Reserved

This **LitPlan** for Karen Cushman's
The Midwife's Apprentice
has been brought to you by Teacher's Pet Publications, Inc.

Copyright Teacher's Pet Publications 1998
11504 Hammock Point
Berlin MD 21811

Only the student materials in this unit plan (such as worksheets,
study questions, and tests) may be reproduced multiple times
for use in the purchaser's classroom.

For any additional copyright questions,
contact Teacher's Pet Publications.

www.tpet.com

TABLE OF CONTENTS - *The Midwife's Apprentice*

Introduction	5
Unit Objectives	8
Reading Assignment Sheet	9
Unit Outline	10
Study Questions (Short Answer)	13
Quiz/Study Questions (Multiple Choice)	21
Pre-reading Vocabulary Worksheets	35
Daily Lessons	51
Nonfiction Assignment Sheet	54
Oral Reading Evaluation Form	62
Writing Assignment 1	53
Writing Assignment 2	64
Writing Assignment 3	71
Speaker	78
Project	57
Writing Evaluation Form	66
Vocabulary Review Activities	79
Extra Writing Assignments/Discussion ?s	73
Unit Review Activities	81
Unit Tests	85
Unit Resource Materials	127
Vocabulary Resource Materials	143

A FEW NOTES ABOUT THE AUTHOR
Karen Cushman

CUSHMAN, Karen (1941-). Karen Lipski Cushman was born into an ethnic, working-class Chicago family. They moved to Los Angeles in 1952. She didn't know that writing was a job, something that real people did with their lives. The type of jobs she knew about were secretary, salesman, or school crossing guard, like her Grandpa. A scholarship to Stanford University sent her off to write depressing poems and irreverent parodies of school songs. She graduated in 1963 with a degree in English and Greek. She wanted to dig for treasures on the Acropolis by moonlight, instead she worked for the telephone company in Beverly Hills, a job she quit. She found other jobs. Quit them all.

While working at the Hebrew Union College in Los Angeles, she met Philip Cushman, married him and moved to Oregon. There he taught, while she wove, made blackberry jam and had a daughter, Leah. They came back to California, both earning further advanced degrees. She currently is the Assistant Director of the Museum Studies Department at John F. Kennedy University in San Francisco, California. She and her husband and daughter, along with two cats, a dog and a rabbit, live in Oakland, California.

Karen considers herself a late bloomer. She is making a new career late in life, writing children's books and having a wonderful time. Over the years she's had lots of book ideas. She'd tell her husband and that would be that. This time when she told him, he said, "Don't tell me. Write it down." So she did and the rest is history. Her three books are the Newbery Honor Book, *Catherine, Called Birdy* (1994), her Newbery Award Winning, *The Midwife's Apprentice* (1995), and her latest, *The Ballad of Lucy Whipple* (1996). The first two take place in medieval times and the most recent one is set during the Gold Rush. She feels that Catherine, Alyce, and Lucy are all her. Karen Cushman claims she knows herself better now than before she began to write.

INTRODUCTION - *Midwife's Apprentice*

This unit has been designed to develop students' reading, writing, thinking, and language skills through exercises and activities related to *The Midwife's Apprentice* by Karen Cushman. It includes nineteen lessons with extra resource materials plus an optional class project.

The **introductory lesson** introduces students to the medieval time period background information mentioned throughout this novel. It also doubles as the first writing assignment for the unit. Following the introductory activity, students are given an explanation of how the activity relates to the book they are about to read. The next lesson following the transition, students are given the materials they will be using during the unit.

The **reading assignments** are approximately twenty pages each; some are a little shorter while others are a little longer. Students have approximately 15 minutes of pre-reading work to do prior to each reading assignment. This pre-reading work involves reviewing the study questions for the assignment and doing some vocabulary work for ten vocabulary words they will encounter in their reading.

The **study guide questions** are fact-based questions; students can find the answers to these questions right in the text. These questions come in two formats: short answer or multiple choice. The best use of these materials is probably to use the short answer version of the questions as study guides for students (since answers will be more complete), and to use the multiple choice version for occasional quizzes. I might be a good idea to make transparencies of your answer keys for the overhead projector.

The **vocabulary work** is intended to enrich students' vocabularies as well as to aid in the students' understanding of the book. Prior to each reading assignment, students will complete a two-part worksheet for 10 vocabulary words in the upcoming reading assignment. Part I focuses on students' use of general knowledge and contextual clues by giving the sentence in which the word appears in the text. Students are then to write down what they think the words mean based on the words' usage. Part II nails down the definitions of the words by giving students dictionary definitions of the words and having students match the words to the correct definitions based on the words' contextual usage. Students should then have an understanding of the words when they meet them in the text.

After each reading assignment, students will go back and formulate answers for the study guide questions. Discussion of these questions serves as a **review** of the most important events and ideas presented in the reading assignments.

After students complete extra discussion questions, there is a **vocabulary review** lesson which pulls together all of the fragmented vocabulary lists for the reading assignments and gives students a review of all of the words they have studied. Following the reading of the book, two lessons are devoted to the **extra discussion questions/writing assignments/activities**. These questions focus on interpretation, critical analysis and personal response, employing a variety of thinking skills and adding to the students' understanding of the novel. These questions are done as a **group activity**. Using the information they have acquired so far through individual work and class discussions, students get together to further examine the text and to brainstorm ideas relating to the themes of the novel.

The group activity is followed by a **reports and discussion/ activity** session in which the groups share their ideas about the book with the entire class; thus, the entire class gets exposed to many different ideas regarding the themes and events of the book.

There are three **writing assignments** in this unit, each with the purpose of informing, persuading, or having students express personal opinions. The first assignment is to inform: students write a composition about one of the background topics assigned in Lesson One in which students will research English medieval history. The second assignment gives students the opportunity to express their personal ideas: students will design and compose a "missing poster" in which an appeal is made for Alyce's return to the village. The third assignment is to give students a chance to persuade: students pretend to be Alyce trying to convince Jane Sharp to accept her back and allow her to continue her apprenticeship.

In addition, there is a **nonfiction reading assignment**. Students are required to read a piece of nonfiction related in some way to *The Midwife's Apprentice*. After reading their nonfiction pieces, students will fill out a worksheet on which they answer questions regarding facts, interpretation, criticism, and personal opinions. During one class period, students make **oral presentations** about the nonfiction pieces they have read. This not only exposes all students to a wealth of information, it also gives students the opportunity to practice **public speaking**.

Another feature of this unit is the **speaker** day. This provides an extension of the theme of midwife care. A professional in this field will be asked to share information and experiences on this topic.

The **review lesson** pulls together all of the aspects of the unit. The teacher is given four or five choices of activities or games to use which all serve the same basic function of reviewing all of the information presented in the unit.

An **optional class project** is included which has students actively involved in recreating an authentic mini-Renaissance Faire.

The **unit test** comes in two formats: all multiple choice-matching-true/false or with a mixture of matching, short answer, and composition. As a convenience, two different tests for each format have been included.

There are additional **support materials** included with this unit. The **unit resource section** includes suggestions for an in-class library, crossword and word search puzzles related to the novel, and extra vocabulary games and worksheets. There is a list of **bulletin board ideas** which gives the teacher suggestions for bulletin boards to go along with this unit. In addition, there is a list of **extra class activities** the teacher could choose from to enhance the unit or as a substitution for an exercise the teacher might feel is inappropriate for his/her class. **Answer keys** are located directly after the **reproducible student materials** throughout the unit. The student materials may be reproduced for use in the teacher's classroom without infringement of copyrights. No other portion of this unit may be reproduced without the written consent of Teacher's Pet Publications, Inc.

UNIT OBJECTIVES *The Midwife's Apprentice*

1. Through reading Karen Cushman's *The Midwife's Apprentice*, students will see the results of and the value of perseverance.

2. Students will determine characters' status as static or dynamic.

3. Students will become familiar with English medieval history.

4. Students will be exposed to the medieval practice of midwifery.

5. Students will become informed in the modern practice of midwifery.

6. Students will demonstrate their understanding of the text on four levels: factual, interpretive, critical and personal.

7. Students will be given the opportunity to practice reading aloud and silently to improve their skills in each area.

8. Students will answer questions to demonstrate their knowledge and understanding of the main events and characters in *The Midwife's Apprentice* as they relate to the author's theme development.

9. Students will enrich their vocabularies and improve their understanding of the novel through the vocabulary lessons prepared for use in conjunction with the novel.

10. The writing assignments in this unit are geared to several purposes:
    a. To have students demonstrate their abilities to inform, to persuade, or to express their own personal ideas
       Note: Students will demonstrate ability to write effectively to <u>inform</u> by developing and organizing facts to convey information. Students will demonstrate the ability to write effectively to <u>persuade</u> by selecting and organizing relevant information, establishing an argumentative purpose, and by designing an appropriate strategy for an identified audience. Students will demonstrate the ability to write effectively to <u>express personal ideas</u> by selecting a form and its appropriate elements.
    b. To check the students' reading comprehension
    c. To make students think about the ideas presented by the novel
    d. To encourage logical thinking
    e. To provide an opportunity to practice good grammar and improve students' use of the English language.

READING ASSIGNMENT SHEET - *The Midwife's Apprentice*

Date to be Assigned	Chapters	Completion Date
	Chapters 1-3	
	Chapters 4-6	
	Chapters 7-9	
	Chapters 10-12	
	Chapters 13-15	
	Chapters 16, 17, Author's Note	

UNIT OUTLINE - *The Midwife's Apprentice*

1 Library Writing Assignment #1 Nonfiction Rdg	2 Introduction PVR Ch. 1-3 Optional Project Description	3 Study? Ch. 1-3 PVR Ch. 4-6	4 Study? Ch.4-6 PVR Ch. 7-9	5 Study? Ch.7-9 Prediction
6 PVR Ch. 10-12 Oral Reading Evaluation	7 Study ?Ch. 10-12 PVR Ch. 13-15	8 Writing Assignment #2	9 Study ?Ch. 13-15 Work Session	10 Writing Conference PVR Ch.16-Author's Note
11 Characterization	12 Study? Ch.16,17, Author's Note Theme	13 Writing Assignment #3	14 Extra Discussion Questions/ Activities	15 Extra Discussion Questions/ Activities
16 Speaker Day	17 Vocabulary Review	18 Review	19 Test	20 Optional Project Renaissance Faire

Key: P = Preview Study Questions   V = Vocabulary Work   R = Read

STUDY GUIDE QUESTIONS

SHORT ANSWER STUDY GUIDE QUESTIONS - *The Midwife's Apprentice*

Chapters 1-3
1. Where was Brat found?
2. Describe Brat.
3. How did Brat feel about herself and the world around her?
4. Give a description of Jane Sharp.
5. Why did Jane Sharp rename "Brat", Beetle?
6. Why didn't Beetle feed the frozen nest of mice to the cat?
7. How did the town boys treat Beetle and the cat?
8. What torture did the boys inflict upon the cat that Beetle spied? How did it end?
9. Tell what chores Beetle does for Jane Sharp.
10. Why did the villagers get angry with Jane? On whom did they take it out?
11. How did Beetle deliberately begin to pick up some midwifery skills?

Chapters 4-6
1. What food item became plentiful in the midwife's cottage that summer?
2. Where and how did Beetle find the answer to the mystery?
3. Why did the miller's wife throw things at Beetle?
4. Why couldn't Jane Sharp attend the Saint Swithin's Day Fair as planned?
5. How did Beetle react to being told she must go in Jane's place to the fair?
6. What did Beetle have to buy? What else did she acquire?
7. A number of positive events happened to Beetle at the fair. What were they?
8. Why does Beetle choose to rename herself Alyce ?
9. What does Beetle name the cat and why?
10. What predicament does Alyce help Will Russet out of at the end of chapter 6?

Chapters 7-9
1. How was Alyce treated in the village after she saved Will?
2. How did Alyce become aware of how the villagers spent their time?
3. What phenomenon appeared within the village that fall?
4. What activities were revealed by the presence of the strange footprints?
5. What did Alyce throw into the river after the baker's wife discovered her husband's folly?
6. Why was Will calling out from a pit to Alyce?
7. Why did Will tell Alyce she had brought him great luck?
8. What did the villagers notice about Alyce in the late fall of that year?
9. How did Alyce startle the town boys when she saw them teasing the cat?
10. Why did Jane desert Joan, the bailiff's wife, during her labor?
11. How was Alyce able to help Joan along in her delivery?
12. How does the bailiff respond to Jane when she returns from the manor for her fee?

13

Short Answer Study Guide Questions - *The Midwife's Apprentice* Page 2

Chapters 10-12
1. How did Alyce begin to learn more of the midwife's skills?
2. When Alyce goes to visit Tansy's calves, what does she find?
3. Where does Alyce send Edward?
4. Why did Emma Blunt request Alyce to deliver her baby?
5. How did Emma Blunt's delivery go?
6. How did Alyce react to her inability to deliver Emma's baby?
7. Where did Alyce go?
8. Whom did Alyce become fascinated with watching at the inn?
9. How does Alyce learn to recognize letters and words?
10. How does Alyce answer Magister Reese's question. "inn girl, what do you want?"

Chapters 13-15
1. What two familiar visitors come to the inn that spring?
2. What information did Jane Sharp share with Magister Reese that Alyce overheard?
3. In what way did Alyce learn the lesson of the "mighty distance between what one imagines and what is" when she travelled to the manor?
4. What chore did Alyce volunteer to do while visiting Edward at the manor?
5. What does Alyce see in her reflection in the river?

Chapters 16,17, Author's Note
1. What does the prosperous-looking man claim is his wife's ailment?
2. What actually is the woman's condition?
3. How does Alyce help the situation?
4. After the ordeal that night, what does Alyce do?
5. What three offers does Alyce get that June from people she knows at the inn?
6. What does Alyce decide she must do?
7. When Alyce returns to Jane's the first time, what is Jane's response?
8. What does Alyce say to Jane the second time that gets her to open her door and let her and the cat in?
9. In medieval England was midwifery an honorable profession?
10. What three things were the mainstays of medieval midwifery?

SHORT ANSWER STUDY GUIDE QUESTION ANSWERS - *The Midwife's Apprentice*

Chapters 1-3

1. Where was Brat found?
    She was found sleeping in a dung heap.

2. Describe Brat.
    She was small, pale, and scrawny; perhaps twelve or thirteen years old.

3. How did Brat feel about herself and the world around her?
    She hoped and expected nothing for herself.

4. Give a description of Jane Sharp.
    She was a woman neither old nor young, but in between; neither fat nor thin, but in between; an important-looking woman with a sharp nose and a sharp glance and wimple starched into sharp pleats.

5. Why did Jane Sharp rename "Brat", Beetle?
    She put her in mind of a dung beetle burrowing in the dung heap.

6. Why didn't Beetle feed the frozen nest of mice to the cat?
    Her heart ached when she thought of the tiny hairless bodies in those strong jaws.

7. How did the town boys treat Beetle and the cat?
    The taunted, pinched, and bedeviled them both

8. What torture did the boys inflict upon the cat that Beetle spied? How did it end?
    They put an eel and the cat together into a sack and threw them into the pond. Beetle rescued the sack, cut it open, then nursed the cat back to health.

9. Tell what chores Beetle does for Jane Sharp.
    She started the fire each morning, swept the cottage floor, roasted the bacon, washed the dishes, sprinkled fleabane, dusted the shelves, and then gathered honey, collected birds, herbs, leeches, and spider webs in the woods. She accompanied the midwife for her births and carried the basket. Afterwards, she was called in to clean out the soiled straw bed and wash the linen.

10. Why did the villagers get angry with Jane? On whom did they take it out?
    They were angry because she was greedy and wouldn't deliver if they couldn't pay anything. They needed the midwife, so they took their anger out on Beetle, needed by no one.

11. How did Beetle deliberately begin to pick up some midwifery skills?
    She began to watch through the windows.

<u>Chapters 4-6</u>
1. What food item became plentiful in the midwife's cottage that summer?
    The midwife's cottage burst forth into bread- soft wheat, crunchy brown oat, and crusty rolls.

2. Where and how did Beetle find the answer to the mystery?
    She secretly awaited in a tree near where she had watched Jane turn off and saw Jane and the baker furiously kissing in the field.

3. Why did the miller's wife throw things at Beetle?
    She was having a difficult birth, and the midwife was unavailable at the time. Beetle had been dragged to help and proved useless.

4. Why couldn't Jane Sharp attend the Saint Swithin's Day Fair as planned?
    She tripped over a pig and broke her ankle.

5. How did Beetle react to being told she must go in Jane's place to the fair?
    The joy in Beetle's heart warmed her insides and lit her face.

6. What did Beetle have to buy? What else did she acquire?
    She was sent to buy leather flasks, nutmeg, pepper, and the water in which a murderer had washed his hands. She also acquired a wooden comb with a cat on it that looked like her cat.

7. A number of positive events happened to Beetle at the fair. What were they?
    She had been winked at, complimented, given a gift, and mistaken for someone who could read.

8. Why does Beetle choose to rename herself Alyce?
    She had been mistaken for someone named Alyce at the fair, who could read.

9. What does Beetle name the cat and why?
    Now that she had a name, he needed one too so she could call him by it. When she rattled off a list of names, he responded with, "Purr."

10. What predicament does Alyce help Will Russet out of at the end of chapter 6?
    Will slipped and tumbled into the churning river while he and his friends were taunting Alyce. His friends tore off, deserting him. Alyce was up in a tree. She crept out on the

branch so that it lowered into the water, and he could grab onto it to raise himself up out of the water. She saved him even though he had been tormenting her.

<u>Chapters 7-9</u>

1. How was Alyce treated in the village after she saved Will?
    Will didn't throw as many stones, or as hard, but otherwise nothing changed.

2. How did Alyce become aware of how the villagers spent their time?
    She had no fear of the night, so she was sent to fetch and carry messages at all hours throughout the village.

3. What phenomenon appeared within the village that fall?
    Strange footprints appeared which everyone thought to be the devil.

4. What activities were revealed by the presence of the strange footprints?
    The villagers' thievery, gluttony, and deceit were revealed wherever the footprints appeared.

5. What did Alyce throw into the river after the baker's wife discovered her husband's folly?
    She threw blocks of wood carved in the shape of hooves.

6. Why was Will calling out from a pit to Alyce?
    His cow, Tansy, was about to deliver her calf and he needed help.

7. Why did Will tell Alyce she had brought him great luck?
    Tansy delivered twins instead of just one calf.

8. What did the villagers notice about Alyce in the late fall of that year?
    She grew in knowledge and skills and they began to ask her *how*, *why*, and *what can I?*

9. How did Alyce startle the town boys when she saw them teasing the cat?
    Upon her return from gathering nuts, she heaved the biggest, hardest, and heaviest nuts at them and threatened them with a devil's potion.

10. Why did Jane desert Joan, the bailiff's wife, during her labor?
    It was a difficult birth, one she assumed would end in stillbirth. Lady Agnes, at the manor, requested Jane, so she went to the manor to deliver Lady Agnes' baby and planned to return to take Joan's dead baby from her later and collect both fees.

11. How was Alyce able to help Joan along in her delivery?
    She gave her all she had of care, courtesy, and hard work.

12. How does the bailiff respond to Jane when she returns from the manor for her fee?
    He tells her that they have no need of her and that her apprentice has taken care of them with her two strong hands and her common sense.

Chapters 10-12

1. How did Alyce begin to learn more of the midwife's skills?
   She stole her way into the shadows of the mothers' cottages and watched the midwife at work closely.

2. When Alyce goes to visit Tansy's calves, what does she find?
   She finds a forlorn, hungry little boy of about six years old asleep in the hay.

3. Where does Alyce send Edward?
   She sends him off to the manor to help with the threshing so he can have a decent life.

4. Why did Emma Blunt request Alyce to deliver her baby?
   She was Joan's (the bailiff's wife's) sister and since Alyce helped Joan, she had to have her.

5. How did Emma Blunt's delivery go?
   Alyce, doubtful and uncertain, sent for the midwife to finish the job.

6. How did Alyce react to her inability to deliver Emma's baby?
   She considered herself a failure and turned her back on all that she knew that had come to be dear to her and headed up the road from the village. The cat went with her.

7. Where did Alyce go?
   She worked at the inn that sat at the crossroad where the road from the village met the road to the sea.

8. Who did Alyce become fascinated with watching at the inn?
   She watched the thin, brown-coated man hunched over a table close to the fire, writing.

9. How does Alyce learn to recognize letters and words?
   Magister Reese pretends to teach Alyce's cat letters, words, and encyclopedic wisdom, but really he is aware that Alyce is taking it all in and knows that she's learning all that he is willing to share.

10. How does Alyce answer Magister Reese's question. "inn girl, what do you want?"
    She tells him that she wants a full belly, a contented heart, and a place in this world.

Chapters 13-15

1. What two familiar visitors come to the inn that spring?
    Will Russet and Jane Sharp both stopped by the inn where Alyce was working.

2. What information did Jane Sharp share with Magister Reese that Alyce overheard.
    Jane told Magister Reese that she needed an apprentice that can try and risk and fail and try again and not give up.

3. In what way did Alyce learn the lesson of the 'mighty distance between what one imagines and what is' when she travelled to the manor?
    She imagined that the boy, Edward, would be desolate and would want to leave with her. In reality, he was content and well fed at the manor.

4. What chore did Alyce volunteer to do while visiting Edward at the manor?
    She helped to scrub the woolly sheep.

5. What does Alyce see in her reflection in the river?
    She sees a clean, pretty girl with all her teeth and limbs and a face unmarked by pock or witchcraft and hope and happiness in her big, dark eyes.

Chapters 16, 17, Author's Note

1. What does the prosperous-looking man claim is his wife's ailment?
    He claims his wife is being devoured by a stomach worm.

2. What actually is the woman's condition?
    She is about to deliver a baby.

3. How does Alyce help the situation?
    She is able to deliver the loud, lusty boy successfully.

4. After the ordeal that night, what does Alyce do?
    She goes outside with Magister Reese and John Dark and laughs a true laugh that comes from her gut.

5. What three offers does Alyce get that June from people she knows at the inn?
    Magister Reese wants her to return to Oxford with him to care for his widowed sister, the rich merchant and his wife want to take her back to Salisbury with them to care for their son, and Jennet offers her a raise to stay at the inn.

6. What does Alyce decide she must do?
    She must return to the village and resume her midwife apprenticeship.

7. When Alyce returns to Jane's the first time, what is Jane's response?
    She will not have her.

8. What does Alyce say to Jane the second time that gets her to open her door and let her and the cat in?
    She tells her that she will try and risk and fail and try again and not give up.

9. In medieval England was midwifery an honorable profession?
    No, because it was practiced by and on women.

10. What three things were the mainstays of medieval midwifery?
    A combination of common sense, herbal knowledge, and superstition.

MULTIPLE CHOICE STUDY GUIDE/QUIZ QUESTIONS- *The Midwife's Apprentice*

Chapters 1-3

1. Brat was found
    a. in a dung heap.
    b. under a layer of leaves and berries.
    c. in a pile of spoiled straw, garbage, and animal droppings.
    d. both a and c

2. Brat was
    a. large-boned and pale.
    b. scrawny and underfed.
    c. twelve or thirteen years old.
    d. both b and c.

3. Brat had a sunny outlook on her life.
    a. true
    b. false

4. Jane Sharp appeared
    a. neither young nor old.
    b. neither fat not thin.
    c. important-looking.
    d. all of the above

5. Jane's new name for Beetle came from
    a. her former apprentice.
    b. where she found her.
    c. what she looked like.
    d. both b and c.

6. Beetle didn't feed the frozen nest of baby mice to the cat because
    a. she was angry with the cat.
    b. the fox got them first.
    c. her heart ached at the thought of it..
    d. the cat needed to eat only cheese.

7. The town boys could be counted on to
    a. torment and tease Beetle and the cat.
    b. help Beetle out when she needed it.
    c. do odd jobs for Jane Sharp.
    d. play tag day in and out.

Study Guide/Quiz Questions *The Midwife's Apprentice* Multiple Choice Format Page 2

8. Beetle was able to rescue the cat from the eel torture.
    a. false
    b. true

9. Jane Sharp took in Beetle because
    a. she was cheap labor.
    b. she appeared too stupid to be of any competition.
    c. she was scared and ignorant.
    d. all of the above

10. Which of the following was *not* one of Beetle's chores?
    a. washing the dishes.
    b. starting the fire.
    c. collecting the rain water.
    d. roasting the bacon.

11. Jane Sharp was a generous and compassionate midwife.
    a. true
    b. false

12. Beetle began to learn midwifery by
    a. watching through the windows.
    b. peeking from a dark corner within the cottage.
    c. taking notes during the delivery.
    d. talking to the mothers after the births.

Study Guide/Quiz Questions *The Midwife's Apprentice* Multiple Choice Format Page 3

<u>Chapters 4-6</u>
1. Which food item did not appear in the midwife's cottage early that summer?
    a. rolls.
    b. oatmeal.
    c. wheat bread.
    d. oat bread.

2. Beetle followed Jane Sharp and discovered
    a. she had another job.
    b. she was hiding food in an open air pantry.
    c. her and the miller kissing in a field.
    d. her and the baker kissing in a field off the Old North Road..

3. The miller's wife was upset with Beetle because
    a. Jane was gone when she had promised to be there for her delivery.
    b. Beetle couldn't deliver her baby.
    c. Jane sent the wrong herbs.
    d. she brought the wrong basket for Jane.

4. Jane could not attend the Saint Swithin's Day Fair due to
    a. a loose pig.
    b. a broken leg.
    c. a broken ankle.
    d. both a and c

5. Beetle was disappointed to be made to go to the fair in Jane's place.
    a. false
    b. true

6. What item did Beetle *not* acquire at the fair?
    a. murderer's wash water
    b. flasks
    c. a hairbrush
    d. nutmeg

7. At the fair, Beetle was
    a. mistaken for someone who could read.
    b. winked at.
    c. given a gift.
    d. all of the above

Study Guide/Quiz Questions *The Midwife's Apprentice* Multiple Choice Format Page 4

8. Beetle changes her name to
   a. Janet
   b. Alicia
   c. Alyce
   d. Grommet

9. The cat is named Purr by Alyce because
   a. it is his only response when she rattles off a list of names.
   b. she can spell it.
   c. she feels he must have a name now, too.
   d. both a and c

10. Alyce helps Will Russet by
    a. sneaking food to him secretly.
    b. rescuing him from drowning.
    c. hiding him from the angry miller.
    d. defending him against the bullies.

Study Guide/Quiz Questions *The Midwife's Apprentice* Multiple Choice Format Page 5

<u>Chapters 7-9</u>

1. The village respected and valued Alyce's feat of bravery for Will.
    a. false
    b. true

2. Alyce became aware of how the villagers spent their time because
    a. she was sent to fetch and deliver messages at all times of day and night.
    b. she had no fear of the shadows.
    c. she learned how to listen well.
    d. she was observant when she helped deliver babies.

3. What phenomenon appeared within the village early that fall?
    a. Strange footprints that resembled a weasel.
    b. Odd footprints resembling those of a boar.
    c. Strange footprints thought to be those of the devil.
    d. none of the above

4. Select the one activity *not* discovered by following the strange footprints.
    a. the baker's unfaithfulness
    b. Jane Sharp's greediness
    c. Wat's gluttony
    d. the miller's thievery

5. After the baker's wife discovered her husband's folly, Alyce threw _____ into the river.
    a. herbs and salt
    b. one of Jane's concoctions
    c. blocks of wood carved in the shape of hooves
    d. some of the baker's rolls

6. Will was calling out for Alyce because
    a. he wanted to apologize to her for his earlier pranks.
    b. he was looking for his missing cow.
    c. he was in trouble with his pals.
    d. he needed her help with Tansy, who fell in a pit and was about to deliver.

7. Tansy successfully delivered twin calves, even although one of them died.
    a. true
    b. false

8. Which question *didn't* the villagers begin to ask Alyce late that fall?
    a. Why?
    b. When?
    c. How?
    d. What can I?

25

Study Guide/Quiz Questions *The Midwife's Apprentice* Multiple Choice Format Page 6

9. When Alyce saw the town boys teasing the cat, she threw nuts at them and threatened them. How did they respond?
    a. The laughed at her.
    b. They threw nuts back at her.
    c. They were startled and unable to move.
    d. The held the cat hostage.

10. Jane Sharp deserted Joan, the bailiff's wife, in her labor because
    a. Joan was uncooperative.
    b. Lady Agnes, at the manor, needed her at the same time.
    c. she assumed Joan's baby would be stillborn.
    d. both b and c

11. Which item did Alyce *not* use to help Joan along with her birth?
    a. spells and magic
    b. hard work
    c. care
    d. courtesy

12. When Jane returns to the bailiff's for her fee
    a. she is paid one half of her requested amount.
    b. she is told Joan and the baby have died.
    c. She's told she was not needed.
    d. Alyce is cowering in fear in the corner.

Study Guide/Quiz Questions *The Midwife's Apprentice* Multiple Choice Format Page 7

<u>Chapters 10-12</u>

1. After delivering, Alyce Little, Joan, the bailiff's wife's baby, Alyce thought she knew most of what she needed to know about delivering babies.
    a. true
    b. false

2. When Alyce goes to visit Tansy's calves she finds
    a. Will crying because one of the calves died.
    b. that one of the calves has run off.
    c. Tansy has run off with the calves.
    d. a forlorn sleeping boy of about six years old.

3. Alyce sends Edward to
    a. the miller to learn grinding.
    b. the manor to help with the threshing.
    c. the baker to learn kneading of the dough.
    d. the smith to learn shoeing of the horses.

4. Emma Blunt requested Alyce to deliver her baby because
    a. she had delivered her sister's baby.
    b. she was angry over Jane's greed.
    c. Alyce was highly regarded by all of the town.
    d. Alyce was a distant relative.

5. Alyce easily delivered Emma Blunt's baby.
    a. false
    b. true

6. After Emma's baby's birth, Alyce
    a. feels like she has been successful once again.
    b. asks for Jane and Emma's forgiveness
    c. believes she is a nothing.
    d. cries aloud in sadness.

7. Alyce left Emma's cottage and went to
    a. the inn at the crossroads.
    b. the seaside.
    c. the dung heap.
    d. the manor where she had sent Edward hoping for a new job for herself.

Study Guide/Quiz Questions *The Midwife's Apprentice* Multiple Choice Format Page 8

8. Whom does Alyce begin to observe at the inn?
   a. John Dark
   b. Magister Richard Reese
   c. Will Russet
   d. Jennet Dark

9. Alyce is able to learn how to read and write at the inn.
   a. true
   b. false

10. Which of the following *doesn't* Alyce answer when asked by Magister Reese, "what do you want, inn girl?"
    a. a place in this world
    b. a contented heart
    c. a fully belly
    d. a yellow ribbon for my black hair

Study Guide/Quiz Questions *The Midwife's Apprentice* Multiple Choice Format Page 9

<u>Chapters 13-15</u>

1. Which two villagers were visitors that spring at the inn where Alyce worked?
   a. Will Russet
   b. Emma Blunt
   c. Jane Sharp
   d. Joan, the bailiff's wife
   e. both a and c
   f. both b and d

2. Jane Sharp told Magister Reese that her former apprentice had failed.
   a. false
   b. true

3. Edward is excited to leave the manor and come to the inn with Alyce.
   a. true
   b. false

4. While visiting Edward at the manor, Alyce
   a. scrubbed floors.
   b. scrubbed sheep
   c. scrubbed walls
   d. none of the above

5. When Alyce looks at her reflection in the river she
   a. is pleased.
   b. is disappointed
   c. is fearful.
   d. is confused.

Study Guide/Quiz Questions- *The Midwife's Apprentice* Multiple Choice Format Page 10

<u>Chapters 16, 17, Author's Note</u>
1. The prosperous-looking inn visitor claims his wife
    a. has a stomach worm.
    b. is barren.
    c. has grown stout from too many potpies.
    d. Both a and b

2. In reality, the woman
    a. is about to give birth.
    b. has a tape worm.
    c. ate a spicy dinner.
    d. none of the above

3. Alyce gets involved in the visitors' situation by
    a. putting clean sheets on their bed.
    b. delivering their son.
    c. praying for the saints for the woman.
    d. offering to bring them ale and bread.

4. Alyce affirms herself that evening after the ordeal by
    a. laughing a true, gut laugh.
    b. drinking a stout ale.
    c. finally crying.
    d. none of the above

5. Who of the following does *not* make Alyce an offer that June?
    a. Jane Sharp
    b. Jennet Dark
    c. Magister Reese
    d. the rich merchant and his wife

6. Whose offer *does* Alyce accept?
    a. Jennet Dark's
    b. Magister Reese's
    c. the rich merchant's
    d. none of the above

7. Jane Sharp welcomes Alyce back with open arms.
    a. true
    b. false

Study Guide/Quiz Questions *The Midwife's Apprentice* Multiple Choice Format Page 11

8. In order to get Jane Sharp to accept her back, Alyce had to promise to
    a. roast the snails better.
    b. try and risk and fail and try again.
    c. collect only the heaviest nuts and acorns.
    d. not steal her mothers way from her.

9. Midwifery in medieval England was an honorable profession.
    a. false
    b. true

10. Which of the following was *not* a mainstay of medieval midwifery?
    a. superstition
    b. common sense
    c. medical knowledge
    d. herbal knowledge

ANSWER KEY- Multiple Choice Study Guide Questions
The Midwife's Apprentice

Ch.1-3	Ch-4-6	Ch. 7-9
1. D	1. B	1. A
2. D	2. D	2. A
3. B	3. B	3. C
4. D	4. D	4. B
5. D	5. A	5. C
6. C	6. C	6. D
7. B	7. D	7. B
8. D	8. C	8. B
9. C	9. D	9. C
10. B	10. B	10. D
11. A		11. A
		12. C

Ch. 10-12	Ch. 13-15	Ch. 16, 17 Author's Note
1. B	1. E	1. D
2. D	2. A	2. A
3. B	3. B	3. B
4. A	4. B	4. A
5. A	5. A	5. A
6. C		6. D
7. A		7. B
8. B		8. B
9. A		9. A
10. D		10. C

PREREADING VOCABULARY WORKSHEETS

VOCABULARY - *The Midwife's Apprentice* Chapters 1-3

Part I: Using Prior Knowledge and Contextual Clues

Below are the sentences in which the vocabulary words appear in the text. Read the sentence. Use any clues you can find in the sentence combined with your prior knowledge, and write what you think the underlined words mean on the lines provided.

1. An important-looking woman, with a sharp nose and a sharp glance and a *wimple* starched into sharp pleats.
   _____

2. But the girl noticed and, on that frosty night, burrowed deep into the warm, rotting muck, *heedless* of the smell.
   _____

3. "You're not dead. No need to call the *bailiff* to cart you off. Now out of the heap and away."
   _____

4. So Brat, newly *christened* Beetle, got up, and the sharp lady found some work for her to do.
   _____

5. Boys. In every village there were boys, teasing, *taunting*, pinching, kicking.
   _____

6. She did not, and suffered their pinching and poking and spitting in silence, lest her *resistance* inspire them to greater torments.
   _____

7. She did her job with energy and some skill, but without care, *compassion*, or joy.
   _____

8. Beetle carried the basket with the clean linen, ragwort and columbine seeds to speed the birth, and cobwebs for *stanching* the blood.
   _____

9. Beetle began to think perhaps she was kept out not because she was stupid, but to keep her in *ignorance* of the midwife's skills and spells.
   _____

Vocabulary *The Midwife's Apprentice* Chapters 1-3 Page 2

10. Beetle found herself doing more and more of the collecting and stewing and brewing, while Jane Sharp spent her time *haggling* over her fees.

___

Part II: Determining the Meaning

Match the vocabulary words to their dictionary definitions. If there are words for which you cannot figure out the definition by contextual clues and by process of elimination, look them up in a dictionary.

___ 1. wimple   A. unmindful
___ 2. heedless   B. mocked; sneered
___ 3. bailiff   C. opposition
___ 4. christened   D. bartering; dickering
___ 5. taunted   E. woman's headcloth drawn in folds about the chin
___ 6. resistance   F. named
___ 7. compassion   G. arresting officer
___ 8. stanching   H. stopping the flow
___ 9. ignorance   I. unawareness; inexperience
___10. haggling   J. sympathy; caring

Vocabulary - *The Midwife's Apprentice* Chapters 4-6

Part I: Using Prior Knowledge and Contextual Clues

Below are the sentences in which the vocabulary words appear in the text. Read the sentence. Use any clues you can find in the sentence combined with your prior knowledge, and write what you think the underlined words mean on the lines provided.

1. At any other time she would have enjoyed the visit, for never had she been in such a *luxurious* dwelling with two rooms downstairs and a loft above and a high soft bed all enclosed by curtains such as the king or the pope must sleep in.
   _____

2., 3. The summer sun, the press of the curious crowd, and the *exertions* of the *reluctant* mother-to-be warmed the room to the point that Beetle felt she was in hell, being attacked by demons, and her screams joined the rest.
   _____

4. The midwife, needing to *replenish* her stores of leather flasks, nutmeg, pepper, and the water in which a murderer had washed his hands, made plans to attend the Saint Swithin's Day Fair.
   _____

5. The joy in Beetle's heart warmed her insides and lit her face, even through the midwife's ranting about lack of wit and the *dire* consequences if she were to lose the silver pennies or spent too much or to come home with the wrong things.
   _____

6. To get to Goblet-Under-Green, Beetle took the road north that followed the river past the mill then *meandered* easterly and northerly until it ended in the glory that was the Saint Swithin's Day Fair in the market square of Goblet-Under-Green.
   _____

7. She laughed at the puppets, wondered at the *soothsayers*, applauded the singers, and cheered for the racing horses.
   _____

8. The merchant's booth was also filled with *sundry* other wares for wondering at.
   _____

9. Beetle handled it with such charming *solemnity* that the merchant took a fancy to the skinny young thing and, with a broad wink, threw the comb with the cat into the pack with the flasks.
   _____

Vocabulary *The Midwife's Apprentice* Chapters 4-6 Page 2

10. " You have *pluck*, Beetle."
_____

Part II: Determining the Meaning - Match the vocabulary words to their dictionary definitions.

___ 11. luxurious   A. rich; fine
___ 12. exertions   B. spirit; spunk
___ 13. reluctant   C. prophets; fortunetellers
___ 14. replenish   D. unwilling
___ 15. dire   E. dreadful; awful
___ 16. meandered   F. efforts; labors
___ 17. soothsayers   G. restock
___ 18. sundry   H. ambled; twisted
___ 19. solemnity   I. many; numerous
___ 20. pluck   J. seriousness

Vocabulary - *The Midwife's Apprentice* Chapters 7-9

Part I: Using Prior Knowledge and Contextual Clues

Below are the sentences in which the vocabulary words appear in the text. Read the sentence. Use any clues you can find in the sentence combined with your prior knowledge, and write what you think the underlined words mean on the lines provided.

1. Robert and Thomas and the priest, whispering *paternosters*, followed the prints all the way to the mill where, crossing themselves, they unlatched the door.
   _____

2.,3. The priest decided Wat's *gluttony* and *deceit* were the fault of the Devil and not of the boy, so Wat's face was not branded, but William Reeve's bad-tempered pigs were in his care.
   _____

4. First they cooked parsnips with sugar and spices and yeast and poured this into casks, where the *fermenting* mixture sang loud and sweet as it turned into wine.
   _____

5. Then Alyce, with baskets tied to each end of a pole, walked with the cat to the *abbey* gardens to gather fallen fruit.
   _____

6. She couldn't see the figure on the bed at first for all the smoke, and then realized that the *writhing* mound was Joan, the bailiff's proud wife.
   _____

7. Suddenly, the proud reasonable Joan became again the moaning, *mewling* mound.
   _____

8. Then, as the hot pains invaded her body, she shouted and *thrashed* and flailed, shrieking and kicking.
   _____

9. . . . and *henceforth* each of you will giggle like a woman and wear dresses like a woman and give birth like a woman!"
   _____

Vocabulary *The Midwife's Apprentice* Chapters 7-9 Page 2

10. So it was in the middle of the night, when the monks were rising from their beds for midnight prayers, and in the towns <u>revelers</u> were returning full of beef and wine, Joan, with the kind attention of the midwife's apprentice, brought forth a daughter, feet first but perfectly formed, whom she called Alyce Little.

Part II: Determining the Meaning - Match the vocabulary words to their dictionary definitions.

___ 21. paternosters   A. excessive overeating
___ 22. gluttony   B. turning and twisting from pain
___ 23. deceit   C. drinkers; carousers
___ 24. fermenting   D. whimpering; whining
___ 25. abbey   E. monastery; convent
___ 26. writhing   F. ripening
___ 27. mewling   G. parts of the Lord's prayer
___ 28. thrashed   H. dishonesty
___ 29. henceforth   I. tossed violently about
___ 30. revelers   J. from this time on

Vocabulary - *The Midwife's Apprentice* Chapters 10-12

Part I: Using Prior Knowledge and Contextual Clues

Below are the sentences in which the vocabulary words appear in the text. Read the sentence. Use any clues you can find in the sentence combined with your prior knowledge, and write what you think the underlined words mean on the lines provided.

1. They are hiring boys to help with the *threshing*.
___

2. She thought not of her tasks but of Edward's face and the *abundance* of bread and cheese.
___

3. "Such *treachery*! Such thievery! Eating my bread and stealing my mothers! Go!"
___

4., 5. All was chaos, noise and heat and blood, until finally over the *tumult* Alyce could hear the cries of the baby, the moans of the mother, and the laughter of the *triumphant* midwife.
___

6. Jennet could carve a fowl with one hand, turn cream into butter with the other, and still have one left to *hoist* a noisy guest by his shirt and chuck him out the door.
___

7. He had long watched her and wondered what could so *blight* a person so young.
___

8. Magister Reese, it was said, was a *renowned* scholar.
___

9. "This is my master-work, an encyclopaedic *compendium* .
___

Vocabulary *The Midwife's Apprentice* Chapters 10-12 Page 2

10. The cat lost patience with the tutoring and began to bite at the *tantalizingly* moving pen.
_____

11. She learned about the four humors that govern the body, how to plant corn by moonlight, and where the *Antipodes* are.
_____

Part II: Determining the Meaning - Match the vocabulary words to their dictionary definitions.

___ 31. threshing   A. plenty
___ 32. abundance   B. curse
___ 33. treachery   C. fascinatingly
___ 34. tumult   D. beating the grain to separate the seeds from the stalk
___ 35. triumphant   E. lift up
___ 36. hoist   F. famous
___ 37. blight   G. betrayal; disloyalty
___ 38. renowned   H. turmoil
___ 39. compendium   I. uninhabited islands S. E. of New Zealand
___ 40. tantalizingly   J. victorious
___ 41. Antipodes   K. a comprehensive summary

Vocabulary - *The Midwife's Apprentice* Chapters 13-15

Part I: Using Prior Knowledge and Contextual Clues
Below are the sentences in which the vocabulary words appear in the text. Read the sentence. Use any clues you can find in the sentence combined with your prior knowledge, and write what you think the underlined words mean on the lines provided.

1. "Skinning rabbits and sweeping the floors and mucking out the *privy*."
   _____

2. Alyce's face grew hot and then as cold as bare feet in January; her throat tickled and her eyes stung as she imagined the midwife telling Magister Reese of the girl's stupidity, her *incompetence*, and her failure.
   _____

3. "I am *desolate* here without you and as well am starving and beaten and forced to sleep outside."
   _____

4. She *tweaked* Edward's nose and pulled a speckled feather from his hair.
   _____

5. "We will pretend we are about to have a great battle with the Scots but we don't mind for we are sure to be *victorious*."
   _____

6. Before Alyce could *reassure* him that she was there to rescue him and all would be well, he continued, " You haven',t have you, Alyce?"
   _____

7. Fleeces clean, the sheep swam to the bank and scrambled out of the water, *nimble* as goats and hungry as pigs.
   _____

Vocabulary *The Midwife's Apprentice* Chapters 13-15 Page 2

Part II: Determining the Meaning - Match the vocabulary words to their dictionary definitions.

___ 42. privy   A. an outhouse
___ 43. incompetence   B. encourage; inspire
___ 44. desolate   C. successful
___ 45. tweaked   D. deserted; abandoned
___ 46. victorious   E. a sharp pull or twist
___ 47. reassure   F. lively; quick
___ 48. nimble   G. stupidity; inability

Vocabulary *The Midwife's Apprentice* Chapters 16,17 Author's Note

Part I: Using Prior Knowledge and Contextual Clues
    Below are the sentences in which the vocabulary words appear in the text. Read the sentence. Use any clues you can find in the sentence combined with your prior knowledge, and write what you think the underlined words mean.

1. Just then a party of riders rode into the inn yard including a *prosperous*-looking man wearing too much jewelry.
    _____

2. The man lifted the *stout* lady down and they hurried into the inn.
    _____

3. Their attendants were a man and woman, *sullen* and not too bright looking.
    _____

4. So for a time the inn *resounded* with the rumble of the thunder.
    _____

5., 6. The *stupefied* father took the baby to his mother, who commenced scolding and *berating* the little fellow.
    _____

7. She felt again the *vigorous*, squirming, wonderful aliveness of the merchant's son as he wriggled into her hands.
    _____

8. Things were done the way they had long been done, with little *innovation* or progress.
    _____

9. If these practices helped, it was not through magical intervention, but because of the calming and strengthening effect of the midwife and mother's faith in their *efficacy.*
    _____

Vocabulary *The Midwife's Apprentice* Chapters 16,17& Note Page 2

10. With the increased participation of doctors in the birth process, midwives fell into *disrepute*, but since the 1960's there has been renewed interest in midwifery in this country and elsewhere.

_____

Part II: Determining the Meaning - Match the vocabulary words to their dictionary definitions.

___ 49. prosperous   A. heavy set
___ 50. stout   B. dishonor
___ 51. sullen   C. an improvement
___ 52. resounded   D. energetic
___ 53. stupefied   E. silent
___ 54. berating   F. well-to-do
___ 55. vigorous   G. echoed
___ 56. innovation   H. scolding
___ 57. efficacy   I. astonished; shocked
___ 58. disrepute   J. effectiveness; capability

ANSWER KEY: VOCABULARY - *The Midwife's Apprentice*

Ch. 1-3	Ch. 4-6	Ch. 7-9	Ch. 10-12
1. E	11. A	21. G	31. D
2. A	12. F	22. A	32. A
3. G	13. D	23. H	33. G
4. F	14. G	24. F	34. H
5. B	15. E	25. E	35. J
6. C	16. H	26. B	36. E
7. J	17. C	27. D	37. B
8. H	18. I	28. I	38. F
9. I	19. J	29. J	39. K
10. D	20. B	30. C	40. C
			41. I

Ch. 13-15	Ch. 16, 17 Author's Note
42. A	49. F
43. G	50. A
44. D	51. E
45. E	52. G
46. C	53. I
47. B	54. H
48. F	55. D
	56. C
	57. J
	58. B

DAILY LESSONS

LESSON ONE

Objectives
1. To provide students the opportunity to gather information about medieval times
2. To give students the opportunity to fulfill their nonfiction reading assignment that goes along with this unit
3. To give students practice using library resources
4. To prepare students for the introductory activity in Lesson Two.
5. To give students the opportunity to write to inform by developing and organizing facts to convey information.

Activity

Assign one of the topics on the following page to each of your students. Some topics will require a pair of students, or a small group to research. Distribute Writing Assignment #1. Discuss the directions in detail. Take your students to the library so they may work on the assignment. Students should fill out a "Nonfiction Assignment Sheet" for at least one of the sources they used, and students should submit these sheets with their compositions.

RESEARCH TOPICS - *The Midwife's Apprentice*

1. What dates comprise the medieval time period historically?
2. What traditions and practices (including midwifery) were common during this time?
3. Of what importance were Saints in this time period?
4. Research the following Saints and the origin of their names and their domains. Saint Cuthbert, Saint Giles, Saint Margaret, Saint Dingad, Saint Vigor, Saint Anthony, Saint Mildred, Saint Polycarp, Saint Felicitas, Saint Loy and any others.
5. How were herbs and plants used during this time period?
6. Research the following herbs and their common and medicinal uses during this time period and their use today. Belladonna, nightshade, poppy, smut rye, black alder tree, borage leaves, birthwort roots, nutmeg, black currants, leeks, wormwood, comfrey leaves, ragwort, columbine, bryony, cumin, cecily, cowslip, sage, mistletoe, elder leaves, milkwort, henbane, nettle, feverfew, and mallows.
7. How did men, women, and children dress during this time period?
8. How much education did the typical person have in this time period?
9. Where animals viewed differently than they are in our society today? If so, how?
10. Research the uses for the following animal parts during this time period: leeches, cobwebs, snail jelly, goat's beard, dragon dung, mouse ears, frog liver, toad ashes, etc.
11. What jobs or professions were most common during this time period?
12. Where did names originate during this time? Research to determine how the following probably came to be: Gilbert Gray-Head, Thomas -At- the- Bridge, William the Reeve, Roger Mustard, Alnoth the Saxon, Annie Broadbeam, Emma and Matthew Blunt, Jennett and John Dark, Thomas the Stutterer, Robert Weaver, Joan-At-the -Bridge, Walter the Blacksmith, Steven the Fletcher, Grommett Smith, and Cab the Groom.
13. What was the average life expectancy in medieval times?
14. How were gems valued during this time period? List their more unusual uses.
15. Explain the origin of and how the following holidays were celebrated: Lady Day, Mayday, Corpus Christi Day, Saint John's Eve, Martinmas, Saint Swithin's Day, All Hallow's Eve, and Walpurgis Night.
16. What role did religion and superstitions play in everyday life in medieval times?

WRITING ASSIGNMENT #1 - *The Midwife's Apprentice*

PROMPT

You are going to read a story about a young girl your age who faces a tremendous personal challenge in a very different time. It is realistic or historical fiction (the events in the novel *could* have taken place, but the characters and events are *fictional*). Before you read it, however, you should have some background information about some of the places and things mentioned in the story.

You have been assigned one topic about which you must find information. You are to read as much as you can about that topic and write a composition in which you relate what you have learned from your reading. Note that this is a *composition*, not just a sentence or two.

PREWRITING

You will go to the library. When you get there, use the library's resources to find information about your topic. Look for books, encyclopedias, articles in magazines- anything that will give you the information you require. Take a few notes as you read to help you remember important dates, names, places, or other details that will be important in your composition.

After you have gathered information and become well-read on the subject of your report, make a little outline, putting your facts in order.

DRAFTING

You will need an introductory paragraph in which you introduce your topic.

In the body of your composition, put the "meat" of your research- the facts you found- in paragraph form. Each paragraph should have a topic sentence (a sentence letting the reader know what the paragraph will be about) followed by an explanation, examples or details.

Write a concluding paragraph in which you summarize the information you found and conclude your report.

PROMPT

After you have finished a rough draft of your paper, revise it yourself until you are happy with your work. Then, ask a student who sits near you to tell you what he/she likes best about your work, and what things he/she thinks can be improved. Take another look at your composition, keeping in mind your critic's suggestions, and make the revisions you feel are necessary.

PROOFREADING

Do a final proofreading of your paper double-checking your grammar, spelling, organization, and the clarity of your ideas.

NONFICTION ASSIGNMENT SHEET - *Midwife's Apprentice*
(To be completed after reading the required nonfiction article)

Name _____ Date _____

Title of Nonfiction Read _____

Written By _____ Publication Date _____

I. Factual Summary: Write a short summary of the piece you read.

II. Vocabulary
    1. With which vocabulary words in the piece did you encounter some degree of difficulty?

    2. How did you resolve your lack of understanding with these words?

III. Interpretation: What was the main point the author wanted you to get from reading his work?

IV. Criticism
    1. With which points of the piece did you agree or find easy to accept? Why?

    2. With which points of the piece did you disagree or find difficult to believe? Why?

V. Personal Response: What do you think about this piece? <u>OR</u> How does this piece influence your ideas?

LESSON TWO

Objectives
1. To introduce *The Midwife's Apprentice* unit
2. To check students' nonfiction reading assignments
3. To distribute books and other related materials
4. To model effective oral reading skills by reading aloud chapter 1
5. To have students identify setting and point of view

Activity #1
    Inquire as to what level of knowledge your class now has concerning medieval history and the practice of midwifery. Allow time for students to share whatever information they may have had or have learned from their earlier research on these two topics. Ask if any of them have visited a Renaissance Faire. If so, have them share any experiences they are willing to share with the class about the events and happenings at one of those. Ask if any of them or anyone they know was delivered by a midwife. What is a midwife? How is a midwife different from a doctor? Tell students that in the book they'll be reading, a young girl close to their age, is in a desperate situation and becomes a medieval midwife's apprentice, quite by accident.

Activity #2
    Distribute the materials students will use in this unit. Explain in detail how students are to use these materials.

    Study Guides Students should preview the study guide questions before each reading assignment to get a feeling for what events and ideas are important in that section. After reading the section, students will (as a class or individually) answer the questions to review the important events and ideas from that section of the book. Students should keep the study guides as study materials for the unit test.

    Vocabulary Prior to reading a reading assignment, students will do vocabulary work related to the section of the book they are about to read. Following the completion of the reading of the book, there will be a vocabulary review of all the words used in the vocabulary assignments. Students should keep their vocabulary work as study materials for the unit test.

    Reading Assignment Sheet You need to fill in the reading assignment sheet to let students know when their reading has to be completed. You can either write the assignment sheet on a side blackboard or bulletin board and leave it there for students to see each day, or you can make copies for each student to have. In either case, you should advise students to become very familiar with the reading assignments so they know what is expected of them.

Extra Activities Center The Unit Resources portion of this unit contains suggestions for a library of related books and articles in your classroom as well as crossword and word search puzzles. Make an extra activities center in your room where you will keep these materials for students to use. (Bring the books and articles in from the library and keep several copies of the puzzles on hand.) Explain to students that these materials are available for students to use when they finish reading assignments or other class work early

Books Each school has its own rules and regulations regarding student use of school books. Advise students of the procedures that are normal for your school.

Activity #3

Have students examine the cover of the book commentary and then turn to page 1. Read this and the next four pages to them as they follow along. Identify the use of third person narration and begin to gather details to predict setting. Emphasize earlier covered items presented now within the context. Encourage students to close their eyes and try to visualize the scene while you read. Assign P, V, R for this and the next two chapters.

OPTIONAL PROJECT RENAISSANCE FAIRE

This project is separate from the rest of *The Midwife's Apprentice* unit, so you can either use it while you are doing *The Midwife's Apprentice* unit or as a separate mini-unit after you have completed the unit test for the book. Also, having it as a separate project enables you to eliminate it if you want or need to for some reason, without disrupting the normal flow of the unit. (Ideally, your students would attend a Renaissance Faire as suggested in the Extra Activities section of the unit plan which would eliminate most of the first assignment)

Objective

To guide and assist students in demonstrating their knowledge of the medieval era by researching, planning, and recreating an authentic Renaissance Faire.

Assignment 1

Beetle attended the Saint Swithin's Day Fair. Students can review chapter 5 of the book for details to record about the fair. Further research should be encouraged and planned to allow students to get a comprehensive idea of these fairs.

Assignment 2

Determine as a large group the details of your Renaissance Faire. Everything will need to be decided from- the various events, stands, merchants, and foods to -the day and time of the upcoming event.

Assignment 3

Divide the class into smaller groups based upon their interests and your requirements. Within each group, delegate or vote leadership roles. Each group will then need to determine their role in the fair and the tasks that need to be accomplished to be a successful part of the day. A project director or group should be chosen, as well, to oversee that all groups are completing their goals and ultimately pull it all together.

Assignment 4

Give students ample time and available resources to be able to complete their individual roles and group objectives. Readjust assignments or roles as needed. Invite parents, families and friends to share in your final product. This can be a huge undertaking or a min-version. It's your choice dependent upon your available time, resources, and goals.

LESSON THREE

Objectives
1. To review the main ideas and vocabulary from Chapters 1-3
2. To preview study questions and vocabulary from Chapters 4-6

Activity #1

Review the vocabulary from Chapters 1-3 by reproducing the matching section on the chalkboard or on an overhead transparency. Have students volunteer to come up and find the correct match for each vocabulary word. After they have made the match, ask them to use the word in an original sentence. Also have them identify its part of speech.

Activity #2

Discuss the answers to the study questions for Chapters 1-3 in detail. Write the answers on the board or overhead transparency so students can have the correct answers for study purposes. Note: It is a good practice in public speaking and leadership skills for individual students to take charge of leading the discussions of the study questions. Perhaps a different student could go to the front of the class and lead the discussion each day that the study questions are discussed during this unit. Of course, the teacher should guide the discussion when appropriate and be sure to fill in any gaps the students leave.

LESSON FOUR

Objectives
1. To review the main ideas and vocabulary from Chapters 4-6
2. To preview study questions and vocabulary from Chapters 7-9

Activity #1

Review the vocabulary from Chapters 4-6 by asking students to practice using the vocabulary in sentences of their own with a partner. After the practice, use the matching section of the prereading vocabulary sheet for Chapters 4-6 as a quiz.

Activity #2

Make a copy of the Chapters 4-6 study guide questions with answers and the matching vocabulary section. Cut them apart, separating the questions and answers or vocabulary word and definition into two piles. Divide the class into two teams. Give one team the questions (or vocabulary word); the other team the answers (or definition). Divide them up among the players so only one person has one question or answer. Select one team to begin play. One person from that team reads one of the questions or answers. Next, a member from the other team tries to match up with the corresponding response. When it is a correct match, move on to another question. Continue play until all questions are answered correctly.

Activity #3

Assign for students to do the prereading and reading work for Chapters 7-9 prior to the next class period. They may use remaining class time to begin this assignment.

LESSON FIVE

.Objectives
1. To review the main events and vocabulary from Chapters 7-9
2. To make predictions

Activity #1

Review the vocabulary from Chapters 7-9 by dividing the class into small groups. Have students quickly copy the vocabulary words onto blank cards. Next, have them copy the definitions onto separate cards. Turn all the cards over, after mixing them up. Have students take turns flipping two cards over to determine if they are a match. If they are a match, that person gets to keep that pair and gets another turn. Students may look at the vocabulary words in their contextual sentences for help, if needed. Continue play until all words are matched with their definitions. If they are ready for a further challenge, add vocabulary from previous chapters. This is similar to the game Concentration.

Activity #2

Use the multiple choice format of the study guide questions for Chapters 7-9 as a quiz to check that students have done the required reading and to review the main ideas of these chapters. Exchange papers for checking and discuss answers.

Activity #3

Discuss the term "prediction". Practice making some simple ones: like the next day's weather or what a classmate will wear the next day. Ask students to get out a piece of paper. Have students make a prediction about what they think will happen in the following chapters now that Alyce has begun to prove herself

LESSON SIX

Objectives
1. To preview the vocabulary and study questions from Chapters 10-12
2. To give students practice reading orally
3. To evaluate students' oral reading
4. To prove previous predictions

Activity #1
Give students about ten minutes to do the prereading vocabulary work and preview study questions from Chapters 10-12.

Activity #2
Have students read Chapters 10-12 out loud in class. This will serve as a time for you to complete the following oral reading evaluation form for each student reading. You probably know the best way to get readers within your class; pick students at random, ask for volunteers, have students select each other, spin a spinner, etc. Reading of these chapters orally will better prepare your class for Writing Assignment #2 which follows in Lesson 8.

Activity #3
Have students retrieve their earlier predictions. Discuss together. Were they accurate? Perhaps you may want to reward those students who were accurate with some small prize.

ORAL READING EVALUATION - *Midwife's Apprentice*

Name _____ Class____ Date _____

SKILL	EXCELLENT	GOOD	AVERAGE	FAIR	POOR
Fluency	5	4	3	2	1
Clarity	5	4	3	2	1
Audibility	5	4	3	2	1
Pronunciation	5	4	3	2	1
_____	5	4	3	2	1
_____	5	4	3	2	1

Total _____   Grade _____

Comments:

LESSON SEVEN

Objectives
1. To review the main events and ideas and vocabulary from Chapters 10-12
2. To preview study questions and prereading vocabulary work for Chapters 13-15

Activity #1

Have students glance over the vocabulary from Chapters 10-12. Write each of the ten words separately on the chalkboard leaving space beneath each one, or on separate pieces of newsprint taped to the wall around the room. Divide the class into ten teams or pairs. Have each team list as many synonyms for their word as they can come up with, beneath it, on the chalkboard or newsprint. Give them a time limit and reward the team who comes up with the most correct synonyms. It is up to you if you want them to be able to refer to a thesaurus or dictionary first. If class can handle, you could have them give an at least one antonym for their word too.

Activity #2

Review the main ideas and events from Chapters 10-12 by allowing your class to decide in which manner they would like to do that. They could choose from any of the earlier techniques, or devise a new one.

Activity #3

In small groups, have students preview prereading vocabulary and study guide questions for Chapters 13-15. Assign reading of these chapters to be completed by class meeting for Lesson 9.

LESSON EIGHT

Objective

To give students the opportunity to express personal ideas in writing

Activity #1

Distribute Writing Assignment #2 and discuss directions in detail. Give students the remainder of the class time to ask questions and work on this assignment.

WRITING ASSIGNMENT #2 - *The Midwife's Apprentice*

PROMPT
Now that you have read Chapters 10-12, you know that Alyce runs away because she feels she has failed and she is once again, nothing. She ends up at the nearby inn, yet the townspeople do not know what happened to her or where she went. Your assignment is to design a MISSING POSTER appealing for Alyce's immediate return.

PREWRITING
Your poster should carry all the usual information that a MISSING POSTER would contain such as: clarity, appeal, picture of the missing person, picture of her pet, last place seen and direction headed, physical description, including any remarkable features, clothing last seen wearing, persons that can be reached if she is found, and any other information that you feel would help identify Alyce and assist in her speedy return. Your poster must fit on an 8 1/2" by 11" sheet of paper or index paper.

DRAFTING
You need to make a few basic decisions concerning your poster. What size will the graphic representation of the likeness of Alyce be? Will you have a background? What will be the attention-getter in your poster? How can you make all your information appealing for Alyce's return fit on one page? How will you layout or design your poster? How will it look on the page? What type lettering will you use? Once you have decided these things, you can put pencil to paper and make a rough draft of your poster.

PROMPT
When you finish the rough draft of your poster, ask a student who sits near you to look over it. After reviewing your rough draft, he\she should tell you what he\she liked best about your work, and ways in which your work could be improved. Reread your poster considering your critic's comments, and make the corrections you think are necessary.

PROOFREADING
Do a final proofreading of your poster double-checking your grammar, spelling, organization, and the clarity of your ideas.

LESSON NINE

Objectives
1. To review the main events and ideas and vocabulary from Chapters 13-15
2. To give students the opportunity to work on their MISSING POSTERS

Activity #1

Hand out four little slips of paper or mini cards to each student that have the letters A,B,C, or D on them. A good idea is to use different color cards for each letter. Use the multiple choice study guide questions and answers on Chapters 13-15 for an oral review. Read the question (and/ or show it on the overhead). Then give students the four possible answers, labeling them A, B, C, or D (or show on overhead again). Students respond by holding up the card with what they think is the correct answer. This is one variety of Every Student Response. Remind students not to look at what others are holding up, but to simply display the card of their choice. This is a quick indicator of students' comprehension. You can make it somewhat different by requiring complete silence and having them read the questions silently from the overhead, or make it more mysterious (fun?) by blindfolding everyone and have them hold up a certain number of fingers per answer instead of using the cards. You can also review vocabulary in this way by providing students with four possible definition responses per word.

Activity #2

After adequate time has been spent on the earlier activity, allow students to work on or to complete their Missing Posters.

LESSON TEN

Objectives
1. To preview study questions and prereading vocabulary for Chapters 16- Author's Note
2. To give students the opportunity to silently read Chapters 16-Author's Note in class
3. To evaluate students' writing
4. To have students revise their Writing Assignment 1 papers

Activity #1

Assign the prereading vocabulary pages, study guide questions and reading of Chapters 16- Author's Note. Students should work on this independently while they are waiting for their conference with you.

Activity #2

Call students to your desk (or some other private area) to discuss their papers from Writing Assignment 1. Use the following Writing Evaluation Form to help structure your conference. Give students a date when their revisions are due.

WRITING EVALUATION FORM - *The Midwife's Apprentice*

Name _____ Date _____

Writing Assignment #1 for *The Midwife's Apprentice* unit   Grade _____

Circle One For Each Item:

Description (paragraph 1)	excellent	good	fair	poor
Plans (body paragraphs)	excellent	workable	fair	not realistic
Conclusion	excellent	good	fair	poor
Grammar:	excellent	good	fair	poor (errors noted)
Spelling:	excellent	good	fair	poor (errors noted)
Punctuation:	excellent	good	fair	poor (errors noted)
Legibility:	excellent	good	fair	poor

Strengths:

Weaknesses:

Comments/Suggestions:

LESSON ELEVEN

Objectives
1. To identify character traits
2. To determine if a character is static or dynamic
3. To apply characterization technique to other characters

Activity #1
Reproduce the following graphic organizers so that each student has one of each of them. Make an overhead of each for you to use to model how to fill each of the charts out. Using Beetle/Alyce as an example, fill out the character traits chart asking the class for input based on the listed categories. Next, fill out the Static/ Dynamic chart also using Beetle/Alyce as an example of a dynamic character. Lead students to deduct that she is a dynamic character rather than a static character through use of the form. Inform students that they will be working on these graphic organizers for homework. They are to choose two other characters form the novel and fill out both charts on them.

LESSON TWELVE

Objectives:
1. To review the main events and ideas and vocabulary from Chapters 16-Author's Note.
2. To discuss the theme of perseverance

Activity #1
Use the multiple choice format of the study guide questions for Chapters 16-Author's Note as a quiz to check that students have done the required reading and to review the main ideas of these chapters. Exchange papers for checking and discuss answers. Use any earlier vocabulary review exercise to review vocabulary from these chapters.

Activity #2
Write the word perseverance up on the board or overhead. Ask students what they think that big word means. If unaware, allow the use of a dictionary to locate a definition. Divide the class into small groups. Assign each group a set of chapters from the novel. Ask them to locate examples of Beetle/Alyce's perseverance. Taking turns, share and record the groups' findings with the class. Discuss the benefits of practicing this characteristic. Perform short role-playing situations where characters exhibit this quality and situations where it is not present. Discuss the difference in the outcomes of the situations.

LESSON THIRTEEN

Objectives
 To give students the opportunity to write to persuade

Activity #1
 Distribute Writing Assignment #3 and discuss the directions in detail. Give students the remainder of class time to work on this assignment.

Character_____

Physical Traits of Character	Actions of Character	Speech of Character	Thoughts and Feelings of Character	What others say about Character

Static or Dynamic

_____ is a **static/dynamic** character because

Character's Name (circle one)

Beginning Personality	Plot events that may /may not cause change					Ending Personality

WRITING ASSIGNMENT #3 - *The Midwife's Apprentice*

PROMPT

Now that you have finished reading this book, you know that Alyce chooses to leave the inn and returns to Jane Sharp to resume being her apprentice. She is very sure that she wants to do this, now that she has successfully delivered a baby at the inn. The problem she faces is that Jane is unreceptive, at first. Jane does not respond to Alyce's plea the way Alyce expected. Your assignment is to pretend to be Alyce who writes a letter to Jane Sharp defending her position and convincing her to take her back.

PREWRITING

To begin with, create a list of reasons that support your objective of convincing Jane that your return will be the best thing for both of you. Come up with any and all possible arguments you can think of that will promote your choice in this matter. Review the last chapter in the book for some ideas. Decide which are your strongest justifiable arguments, and which are less substantial. Organize your points from weaker to strongest utilizing your facts, opinions, and examples as evidence in support of your argument.

DRAFTING

Begin with an introductory paragraph in which you express your desire to return as Jane's midwife apprentice and how that move will benefit her as well as you. Follow that with one paragraph for each of the main points you have to support your argument to convince Jane to take you back as her midwife apprentice. Fill in each paragraph with your facts, opinions, and examples that support your decision. Then, write an ending paragraph that summarizes and restates your opinion and reinforces how you feel about yourself and your abilities to resume your duties as Jane's midwife apprentice.

PROMPT

When you finish the rough draft of your paper, ask a student who sits near you to read it. After reading your rough draft, he\she should tell you what he\she liked best about your work, which parts were difficult to understand, and ways in which your work could be improved. Reread your paper considering your critic's comments, and make the corrections you think are necessary.

PROOFREADING

Do a final proofreading of your paper double-checking your grammar, spelling, organization, and the clarity of your ideas.

LESSON FOURTEEN

Objectives:
1. To discuss the ideas and themes from *The Midwife's Apprentice* in greater detail
2. To have students exercise their interpretive and critical thinking skills
3. To relate some of the ideas in *The Midwife's Apprentice* to the students' lives

Activity #1

Choose the questions from the Extra Discussion Questions/Writing Assignments which seem most appropriate for your students. A class discussion of these questions is most effective if students have been given the opportunity to formulate answers to the questions prior to the discussion. To this end, you may either have all the students formulate answers to all the questions, divide your class into groups and assign one or more questions to each group, or you could assign one question to each student in your class. The option you choose will make a difference in the amount of class time needed for this activity.

LESSON FIFTEEN

Objectives:
1. To complete discussions begun in Lesson Fourteen
2. To allow students time to complete extra activities of their choice

Activity #1

After students have had ample time to formulate answers to the questions which they started in Lesson Thirteen, begin your class discussion of the questions and the ideas presented by the questions. Be sure students take notes during the discussion so they have information to study for the unit test.

EXTRA DISCUSSION QUESTIONS/WRITING ASSIGNMENTS
The Midwife's Apprentice

Interpretive

1. From what point of view is this story told? How would the story change if told from only one character's point of view?

2. Identify the setting. How does it influence the plot of this novel?

3. What are the main conflicts in the story, and how are they resolved?

4. What is foreshadowing? Give examples of foreshadowing used in *The Midwife's Apprentice*.

5. What part did the herbs and remedies play in the practice of medieval midwifery?

6. Complete a character sketch for Alyce and Jane.

7. Where did many of the townsfolk get their names?

8. Explain the role of each of these supporting characters: Purr, village boys, Will, Jennet, and Magister Reese.

9. Define climax. Next, summarize the main events leading up to **it** and the remaining events after **it** that create the resolution.

10. Locate examples of the English dialect used during medieval times. Did non-educated folks' dialect differ from the dialect of educated folks?

11. How do Magister Reese's and Jennet's offers affect Alyce?

Critical

12. Explain the significance of the title "*The Midwife's Apprentice*".

13. What does Alyce learn about herself from her experiences with the midwife?

14. What causes Alyce to return to the midwife rather than take up her other three offers?

15. Compare and contrast the main character's lifestyle in medieval England to yours.

16. Why do you think Alyce decided to save both the cat and Will, rather than let them die?

The Midwife's Apprentice Extra Discussion Questions page 2

17. Compare Jane and Alyce. Are they alike in any ways?

18. How and why does Alyce change during the course of this novel?

19. For what reason do you think Karen Cushman includes some bad words in this book for young readers?

20. Cite some of the religious references in this novel. Why do you think they were included?

21. Who is responsible for Alyce's success and happiness? Defend your answer.

22. Does Jane Sharp have a right to be angry? to charge unaffordable prices? to bully others? Explain your opinions.

23. Is the story of *The Midwife's Apprentice* believable? Why or why not?

24. Discover what motivated Karen Cushman to write a book about a young woman in medieval England.

25. Why does Karen Cushman include all the superstitions and herbal remedies used during this time period?

26. What universal themes appear in *The Midwife's Apprentice*?

27. Do you agree or disagree with Will who says, "Just because you don't know everything don't mean you know nothing."

28. Why were animal twins valued and considered good luck in those days when human twins appeared to be disregarded?

29. Will Alyce "try and risk and fail and try again? Support your answer.

30. Have you read any other books written by Karen Cushman? How do they compare to *The Midwife's Apprentice*? Which one is your favorite? Why?

31. How is a modern child's life different than a child's life in medieval England?

32. Does Jane Sharp help or hurt Alyce?

The Midwife's Apprentice Extra Discussion Questions page 3

Personal Response

33. Why did the scrawniest and ugliest in town chose to pick on Beetle? How did it make them feel? Is that normal? Can you give some examples of similar behavior based on pecking order?

34. Who do you think the Devil was? What made Alyce come up with such a plan? Have you ever wanted to expose someone such as she was able to in this way? Why?

35. Have you ever had some sort of challenge presented to you like Alyce did ? (to read and write) How did it make you feel when you became successful at it?

36. How did Alyce's visit to the Saint Swithin's Day Fair change her? Has unexpected approval and affirmation ever affected you in this way?

37. If you were Beetle, how would you handle the intimidation by the town boys and townsfolk?

38. How and why did the village boys' reactions to Alyce change? Have you ever been able to stand up for yourself like Alyce did and cause a change like that?

39. Why do you think Alyce reverts back to feeling like she knows nothing and is nothing after her failure with Emma Blunt's delivery? Have you ever been hard on yourself like that?

40. Why did Alyce care for and guide little Edward? What does this tell us about her nature? Do you like to babysit or play with younger children? How does it make you feel?

Quotations

1. "Those who don't work don't eat."

2. "Damn you, cat, breathe and live, you flea-bitten sod, or I'll kill you myself."

3. "Push, you cow. If an animal can do it, you can do it."

4. "And don't you be telling anyone, Beetle, or I'll turn you out in the cold again and break both your knees before I do."

5. "And who would I be telling, then? I don't talk to no one but the cat and he don't care who you are kissin'."

6. "Broken by God's whiskers. Broken."

The Midwife's Apprentice Extra Discussion Questions page 4

7. "This face could belong to someone who can read. And has curls. And could have a lover before nightfall. And this is me."

8. "Get out of my sight, Dung Beetle, before I squash you."

9. "I have a name now, cat, and you must also, so I can call you to breakfast on cold, foggy mornings. I will say some names, and you tell me when I have found the right one."

10. Naw, I be not brave. I did it for else you'd have drowned and gone to Hell, a drunken loudmouth bully like you and I would have helped send you there and I could not have that, now, could I?"

11. "You have pluck, Beetle. You have pluck, Alyce."

12. "I am no midwife for cows, Will Russet."

13. "All shiny they were, and sticky to touch. I did not even know them, but I loved them so much."

14. "Touch that cat again and I will unstop this bottle of rat's blood and viper's flesh and summon the Devil, who will change you into women, and henceforth each of you will giggle like a woman and wear dresses like a woman and give birth like a woman!"

15. "We have no need of you, Jane. Your helper has taken care of us with her two strong hands and her good common sense."

16. "Go then, such treachery! Such thievery! Eating my bread and stealing my mothers! Go!"

17. "I am nothing, I have nothing, I can do nothing and learn nothing. I belong no place. I am too stupid to be a midwife's apprentice and too tired to wander again. I should just lie here in the rain until I die."

18. "Oskins, boskins, chickadee, you are such a help to me that I wish you would stay on awhile."

19. "This, puss, is my masterpiece, an encyclopaedic compendium I call the 'The Great Mirror of the Universe Wherein You Can Find Reflected All of the World's Knowledge, Collected by Myself and dedicated to His Ampleness the Bishop of Chester,' so called for he is ample in all the world's virtues."

20. "And what, inn girl, do *you* want?"

The Midwife's Apprentice Extra Discussion Questions page 5

21. "I know what I want. A full belly, a contented heart, and a place in this world. This is what I want, but it is my misfortune instead to be hungry, out of humor, and too stupid to be a midwife's apprentice."

22. "Thundering toads, I am but a poor woman with this wretched inn and a blind man to care for. I am sure God does not begrudge me my little economies."

23. "And a prettier inn girl the world never saw, or you would be if you ever got that flour and dirt off yer face."

24. "Bah, Alyce. I seen you with Tansy. You got guts and common sense. Just because you don't know everything don't mean you know nothin'"

25. "I need an apprentice who can do what I tell her, take what I give her, who can try and risk and fail and try again and not give up. Babies don't stop their borning because the midwife gives up."

26. "Not really lies, Alyce. I just wanted a sister, for all cook's other children have brothers and sisters. Have you come to take me away? You haven't, have you, Alyce? For I am sore content here and mostly have enough to eat, and when cook is cross with me I sleep with the chickens and pretend. No one chases me away and even Lord Arnulf knows my name."

27. "Jane Sharp! It is I, Alyce, your apprentice. I have come back. And if you do not let me in, I will try again and again. I can do what you tell me and take what you give me, and I know how to try and risk and fail and try again and not give up. I will not go away."

LESSON SIXTEEN

Objectives:
1. To make available a knowledgeable professional resource on midwifery
2. To compose thank you notes

Activity #1

In preparation for this lesson, have students prepare a list of questions about midwifery. Ask them to review the book for ideas or points of interest or curiosity. This could be part of your extra discussion/activities classes.

Activity #2

Contact a local healthcare provider or private agency that is willing to provide a speaker. Do this early enough to allow for busy preplanned schedules. Set the date up with the agency based on your timetable. If at all possible, allow the guest to preview *The Midwife's Apprentice* or summarize for him/her prior to her visit. In this way, the speaker will know from what frame of reference the class, as an audience, is coming.

Activity #3

Have speaker address class on the many aspects of midwifery. Perhaps past anonymous caseload examples could be shared. Encourage class members to share their questions and insights with the speaker.

Activity #4

After the speaker has finished, briefly review components of writing a *thank you* note. Assign these for homework. Perhaps you could generate a creative piece of stationery for students depicting the subject matter using Print Shop or Publisher software. Mail to speaker.

LESSON SEVENTEEN

Objective:
> To review all of the vocabulary work done in this unit

Activity

    Choose one (or more) of the vocabulary review activities and spend your class period as directed in the activity. Some of the materials for these review activities are located in the vocabulary resource section of this unit.

VOCABULARY REVIEW ACTIVITIES

1. Divide your class into two teams and have an old-fashioned spelling or definition bee.
2. Give each of your students (or students in groups of two, three or four) a *Midwife's Apprentice* Vocabulary Word Search Puzzle. The person (group) to find all of the vocabulary words in the puzzle first wins.
3. Give students a *The Midwife's Apprentice* Vocabulary Word Search Puzzle without the word list. The person or group to find the most vocabulary words in the puzzle wins.
4. Use a *The Midwife's Apprentice* Vocabulary Crossword Puzzle. Put the puzzle onto a transparency on the overhead projector (so everyone can see it), and do the puzzle together as a class.
5. Give students a *The Midwife's Apprentice* Vocabulary Matching Worksheet to do.
6. Divide your class into two teams. Use *The Midwife's Apprentice* vocabulary words with their letters jumbled as a word list. Student 1 from Team A faces off against Student 1 from Team B. You write the first jumbled word on the board. The first student (1A or 1B) to unscramble the word wins the chance for his/her team to score points. If 1A wins the jumble, go to student 2A and give him/her a definition. He/she must give you the correct spelling of the vocabulary word which fits that definition. If he/she does, Team A scores a point, and you give student 3A a definition for which you expect a correctly spelled matching vocabulary word. Continue giving Team A definitions until some team member makes an incorrect response. An incorrect response sends the game back to the jumbled-word face off, this time with students 2A and 2B. Instead of repeating giving definitions, to the first few students of each team, continue with the student after the one who gave the last incorrect response on the team. For example, if Team B wins the jumbled-word face-off, and student 5B gave the last incorrect answer for Team B, you would start this round of definition questions with student 6B, and so on. The team with the most points wins!

7. Have students write a story in which they correctly use as many vocabulary words as possible. Have students read their compositions orally. Post the most original compositions on your bulletin board.

LESSON EIGHTEEN

Objective:

To review the main ideas presented in *The Midwife's Apprentice*

Activity #1

Choose one of the review games/activities included in the packet and spend your class period as outlined there. Some materials for these activities are located in the unit resource section of this unit.

Activity #2

Remind students that the Unit Test will be in the next class meeting. Stress the review of the Study Guides and their class notes as a last minute, brush-up review for the unit test.

REVIEW GAMES/ACTIVITIES - *The Midwife's Apprentice*

1. Ask the class to make up a unit test for *The Midwife's Apprentice*. The test should have 4 sections: matching, true/false, short answer, and essay. Students may use 1/2 period to make the test and then swap papers and use the other 1/2 class period to take a test a classmate has devised (open book). You may want to use the unit test included in this packet or take questions from the students' unit tests to formulate your own test.

2. Take 1/2 period for students to make up true and false questions (including the answers). Collect the papers and divide the class into two teams. Draw a big tic-tac-toe board on the chalk board. Make one team X and one team O. Ask questions to each side, giving each student one turn. If the question is answered correctly, that students' team's letter (X or O) is placed in the box. If the answer is incorrect, no mark is placed in the box. The object is to get three marks in a row like tic-tac-toe. You may want to keep track of the number of games won for each team.

3. Take 1/2 period for students to make up questions (true/false and short answer). Collect the questions. Divide the class into two teams. You'll alternate asking questions to individual members of teams A & B (like in a spelling bee). The question keeps going from A to B until it is correctly answered, then a new question is asked. A correct answer does not allow the team to get another question. Correct answers are +2 points; incorrect answers are -1 point.

4. Have students pair up and quiz each other from their study guides and class notes.

5. Give students a *The Midwife's Apprentice* crossword puzzle to complete.

6. Divide your class into two teams. Use *The Midwife's Apprentice* crossword words with their letters jumbled as a word list. Student 1 from Team A faces off against Student 1 from Team B. You write the first jumbled word on the board. The first student (1A or 1B) to unscramble the word wins the chance for his/her team to score points. If 1A wins the jumble, go to student 2A and give him/her a clue. He/she must give you the correct word which matches that clue. If he/she does, Team A scores a point, and you give student 3A a clue for which you expect another correct response. Continue giving Team A clues until some team member makes an incorrect response. An incorrect response sends the game back to the jumbled-word face off, this time with students 2A and 2B. Instead of repeating giving clues to the first few students of each team, continue with the student after the one who gave the last incorrect response on the team. For example, if Team B wins the jumbled-word face-off, and student 5B gave the last incorrect answer for Team B, you would start this round of clue questions with student 6B, and so on.

UNIT TESTS

SHORT ANSWER UNIT TEST #1 - *The Midwife's Apprentice*

I. Matching/Identify

____ 1. SAINT SWITHIN'S   A. Threw things at Beetle for her incompetence

____ 2. DEVIL   B. Ointment for mothers-to-be's aching legs

____ 3. EDWARD   C. Alyse sent him to the manor to do threshing

____ 4. ENCYCLOPAEDIA   D. Midwife's fault

____ 5. MURDERER'S WASH   E. Tansy delivered these

____ 6. BEETLE   F. Magister Reese's book

____ 7. GROMMET SMITH   G. Water sold for remedy

____ 8. PURR   H. Manor folk thought Alyce was Edward's

____ 9. GOOSE GREASE   I. Left mysterious footprints

____ 10. MILLER'S WIFE   J. New name for cat

____ 11. SISTER   K. Jane Sharp christened Brat this

____ 12. TWINS   L. Smith's lardy daughter

____ 13. GREED   M. Jane Sharp's fingernails

____ 14. CLEAN   N. How Will describes Alyce

____ 15. PRETTY   O. Fair held at Goblet-Under-Green

The Midwife's Apprentice Short Answer Unit Test 1 Page 2

II. Short Answer

1. Describe Brat and how she felt about herself and the world around her.

2. Give a description of Jane Sharp.

3. How did the town boys treat Beetle and the cat?

4. Tell what chores Beetle does for Jane Sharp.

5. Why did the villagers get angry with Jane? On whom did they take it out?

6. Why did the miller's wife throw things at Beetle?

7. Why couldn't Jane Sharp attend the Saint Swithin's Day Fair as planned and how did Beetle react to being told she must go in Jane's place to the fair?

The Midwife's Apprentice Short Answer Unit Test 1 Page 3

8. A number of positive events happened to Beetle at the fair. What were they?

9. How did Alyce become aware of how the villagers spent their time?

10. What activities were revealed by the presence of the strange footprints?

11. How did Alyce startle the town boys when she saw them teasing the cat?

12. Why did Jane desert Joan, the bailiff's wife, during her labor?

13. How did Alyce begin to learn more of the midwife's skills?

14. Why did Emma Blunt request Alyce to deliver her baby?

15. How does Alyce learn to recognize letters and words?

The Midwife's Apprentice Short Answer Unit Test 1 Page 4

16. How does Alyce answer Magister Reese's question. "inn girl, what do you want?'

17. What information did Jane Sharp share with Magister Reese that Alyce overheard.

18. After the ordeal with the rich merchant and his wife at the inn that night, what does Alyce do?

19. What does Alyce say to Jane the second time that gets her to open her door and let her and the cat in?

20. What three things were the mainstays of medieval midwifery?

The Midwife's Apprentice Short Answer Unit Test 1 Page 5

III. Essay

    Do you agree or disagree with Will who says, "Just because you don't know everything don't mean you know nothing." Explain what he means by this.

IV. Vocabulary

    Listen to the vocabulary words and spell them. After you have spelled all the words, go back and write down the definitions.

1.

2.

3.

4.

5.

6.

7.

8.

9.

10.

KEY: SHORT ANSWER UNIT TEST #1 - *The Midwife's Apprentice*

I. Matching/Identify

O - 1. SAINT SWITHIN'S   A. Threw things at Beetle for her incompetence

I - 2. DEVIL   B. Ointment for mothers-to-be's aching legs

C - 3. EDWARD   C. Alyse sent him to the manor to do threshing

F - 4. ENCYCLOPAEDIA   D. Midwife's fault

G - 5. MURDERER'S WASH   E. Tansy delivered these

K - 6. BEETLE   F. Magister Reese's book

L - 7. GROMMET SMITH   G. Water sold for remedy

J - 8. PURR   H. Manor folk thought Alyce was Edward's

B - 9. GOOSE GREASE   I. Left mysterious footprints

A - 10. MILLER'S WIFE   J. New name for cat

H - 11. SISTER   K. Jane Sharp christened Brat this

E - 12. TWINS   L. Smith's lardy daughter

D - 13. GREED   M. Jane Sharp's fingernails

M - 14. CLEAN   N. How Will describes Alyce

N - 15. PRETTY   O. Fair held at Goblet-Under-Green

II. Short Answer
1. Describe Brat and how she felt about herself and the world around her.
    She was small, pale, and scrawny; perhaps twelve or thirteen years old. She hoped and expected nothing for herself.

2. Give a description of Jane Sharp.

    She was a woman neither old nor young, but in between; neither fat nor thin, but in between; an important-looking woman with a sharp nose and a sharp glance and wimple starched into sharp pleats.

3. How did the town boys treat Beetle and the cat?

    The taunted, pinched, and bedeviled them both.

4. Tell what chores Beetle does for Jane Sharp.

    She started the fire each morning, swept the cottage floor, roasted the bacon, washed the dishes, sprinkled fleabane, dusted the shelves, and then gathered honey, collected birds, herbs, leeches, and spider webs in the woods. She accompanied the midwife for her births and carried the basket. Afterwards, she was called in to clean out the soiled straw bed and wash the linen.

5. Why did the villagers get angry with Jane? On whom did they take it out?

    They were angry because she was greedy and wouldn't deliver if they couldn't pay anything. They needed the midwife, so they took their anger out on Beetle, needed by no one.

6. Why did the miller's wife throw things at Beetle?

    She was having a difficult birth, and the midwife was unavailable at the time. Beetle had been dragged to help and proved useless.

7. Why couldn't Jane Sharp attend the Saint Swithin's Day Fair as planned and how did Beetle react to being told she must go in Jane's place to the fair?

    She tripped over a pig and broke her ankle. The joy in Beetle's heart warmed her insides and lit her face.

8. A number of positive events happened to Beetle at the fair. What were they?

    She was winked at, complimented, given a gift, and taken for someone who could read.

9. How did Alyce become aware of how the villagers spent their time?

    She had no fear of the night, so she was sent to fetch and carry messages at all hours throughout the village.

10. What activities were revealed by the presence of the strange footprints?

    The villagers' thievery, gluttony, and deceit were revealed wherever the footprints appeared.

11. How did Alyce startle the town boys when she saw them teasing the cat?

    Upon her return from gathering nuts, she heaved the biggest, hardest, and heaviest nuts at them and threatened them with a devil's potion.

12. Why did Jane desert Joan, the bailiff's wife, during her labor?

    It was a difficult birth, one she assumed would end in stillbirth. Lady Agnes, at the manor, requested Jane, so she went to the manor to deliver Lady Agnes' baby and planned to return to take Joan's dead baby from her later and collect both fees.

13. How did Alyce begin to learn more of the midwife's skills?

    She stole her way into the shadows of the mothers' cottages and watched the midwife at work closely.

14. Why did Emma Blunt request Alyce to deliver her baby?

    She was Joan, the bailiff's wife's sister, and since Alyce helped Joan, she had to have her.

15. How does Alyce learn to recognize letters and words?
    Magister Reese pretends to teach Alyce's cat letters, words, and encyclopedic wisdom, but really he is aware that Alyce is taking it all in and knows that she's learning all that he is willing to share.
16. How does Alyce answer Magister Reese's question. "inn girl, what do you want?"
    She tells him that she wants a full belly, a contented heart, and a place in this world.
17. What information did Jane Sharp share with Magister Reese that Alyce overheard.
    Jane told Magister Reese that she needed an apprentice that can try and risk and fail and try again and not give up.
18. After the ordeal with the rich merchant and his wife at the inn that night, what does Alyce do?
    She goes outside with Magister Reese and John Dark and laughs a true laugh that comes from her gut.
19. What does Alyce say to Jane the second time that gets her to open her door and let her and the cat in?
    She tells her that she will try and risk and fail and try again and not give up.
20. What three things were the mainstays of medieval midwifery?
    A combination of common sense, herbal knowledge, and superstition.

III. Essay
   Do you agree or disagree with Will who says, "Just because you don't know everything don't mean you know nothing." Explain what he means by this.
       Answers will vary. Judge according to your own standards.

IV. Vocabulary
   Choose ten of the vocabulary words to read orally for the vocabulary section of this unit test.

SHORT ANSWER UNIT TEST 2 *The Midwife's Apprentice*

I. Matching/Identify

____ 1. PRETTY

____ 2. CAT

____ 3. RED

____ 4. GUTS

____ 5. MAGISTER REESE

____ 6. DUNG HEAP

____ 7. READ

____ 8. FLASKS

____ 9. TANSY

____ 10. HERBS

____ 11. ENCYCLOPAEDIA

____ 12. BEETLE

____ 13. PROSPEROUS MAN

____ 14. BRAT

____ 15. FAILED

A. How Will describes Alyce

B. Jane Sharp christened Brat this

C. Will says Alyce has these

D. Will Russett's hair color

E. Beetle's only companion

F. Warm, rotting muck

G. Wife bore him a son delivered by Alyce at Inn

H. What Alyce felt she did

I. Writer staying at Inn

J. Bartered for at the fair by Beetle

K. Will's mother cow

L. Alyce learned to from Magister Reese

M. Used to treat mothers

N. Knew no home and no mother

O. Magister Reese's book

The Midwife's Apprentice Short Answer Unit Test 2 Page 2

II. Short Answer
1. Where was Brat found?

2. How did Brat feel about herself and the world around her?

3. Give a description of Jane Sharp.

4. Why did Jane Sharp rename "Brat" to "Beetle"?

5. Why didn't Beetle feed the frozen nest of mice to the cat?

6. What torture did the boys inflict upon the cat that Beetle spied? How did it end?

7. How did Beetle deliberately begin to pick up some midwifery skills?

8. What food item became plentiful in the midwife's cottage that summer?

9. What did Beetle have to buy for Jane at the Saint Swithin's Day Fair? What else did she acquire?

The Midwife's Apprentice Short Answer Unit Test 2 Page 3

10. Why does Beetle choose to rename herself Alyce ?

11. What does Beetle name the cat and why?

12. What predicament does Alyce help Will Russet out of near the river?

13. What phenomenon appeared within the village that fall?

14. What activities were revealed by the presence of the strange footprints?

15. Why was Will calling out from a pit to Alyce?

16. What did the villagers notice about Alyce in the late fall of that year?

17. Why did Jane desert Joan, the bailiff's wife, during her labor?

The Midwife's Apprentice Short Answer Unit Test 2 Page 4

18. How was Alyce able to help Joan along in her delivery?

19. How did Alyce react to her inability to deliver Emma's baby?

20. What three offers does Alyce get that June from people she knows at the inn? What does Alyce decide she must do?

III. Essay

When Alyce returns to Jane's she says she's changed. Will Alyce "try and risk and fail and try again? Support your answer.

The Midwife's Apprentice Short Answer Unit Test 2 Page 5

IV. Vocabulary

Listen to the vocabulary word and spell it. After you have spelled all the words, go back and write down the definitions.

1.

2.

3.

4.

5.

6.

7.

8.

9.

10.

KEY: SHORT ANSWER UNIT TEST 2 *The Midwife's Apprentice*

I. Matching

A - 1. PRETTY   A. How Will describes Alyce

E - 2. CAT   B. Jane Sharp christened Brat this

D - 3. RED   C. Will says Alyce has these

C - 4. GUTS   D. Will Russett's hair color

I - 5. MAGISTER REESE   E. Beetle's only companion

F - 6. DUNG HEAP   F. Warm, rotting muck

L - 7. READ   G. Wife bore him a son delivered by Alyce at Inn

J - 8. FLASKS   H. What Alyce felt she did

K - 9. TANSY   I. Writer staying at Inn

M - 10. HERBS   J. Bartered for at the fair by Beetle

O - 11. ENCYCLOPAEDIA   K. Will's mother cow

B - 12. BEETLE   L. Alyce learned to from Magister Reese

G - 13. PROSPEROUS MAN   M. Used to treat mothers

N - 14. BRAT   N. Knew no home and no mother

H - 15. FAILED   O. Magister Reese's book

II. Short Answer

1. Where was Brat found?
    She was found sleeping in a dung heap.
2. How did Brat feel about herself and the world around her?
    She hoped and expected nothing for herself.

3. Give a description of Jane Sharp.
    She was a woman neither old nor young, but in between; neither fat nor thin, but in between; an important-looking woman with a sharp nose and a sharp glance and wimple starched into sharp pleats.
4. Why did Jane Sharp rename "Brat" to "Beetle"?
    She put her in mind of a dung beetle burrowing in the dung heap.
5. Why didn't Beetle feed the frozen nest of mice to the cat?
    Her heart ached when she thought of the tiny hairless bodies in those strong jaws.
6. What torture did the boys inflict upon the cat that Beetle spied? How did it end?
    They put an eel and the cat together into a sack and threw them into the pond. Beetle rescued the sack, cut it open, the nursed the cat back to health.
7. How did Beetle deliberately begin to pick up some midwifery skills?
    She began to watch through the windows.
8. What food item became plentiful in the midwife's cottage that summer?
    The midwife's cottage burst forth into bread- soft wheat, crunchy brown oat, and crusty rolls.
9. What did Beetle have to buy for Jane at the Saint Swithin's Day Fair? What else did she acquire?
    She was sent to buy leather flasks, nutmeg, pepper, and the water in which a murderer had washed his hands. She also acquired a wooden comb with a cat on it that looked like her cat.
10. Why does Beetle choose to rename herself Alyce ?
    She had been mistaken for someone named Alyce at the fair, who could read.
11. What does Beetle name the cat and why?
    Now that she had a name, he needed one too so she could call him by it. When she rattled off a list of names, he responded with, "Purr."
12. What predicament does Alyce help Will Russet out of near the river?
    Will slipped and tumbled into the churning river while he and his friends were taunting Alyce. His friends tore off, deserting him. Alyce was up in a tree. She crept out on the branch so that it lowered into the water, and he could grab onto it to raise himself up out of the water. She saved him even though he had been tormenting her.
13. What phenomenon appeared within the village that fall?
    Strange footprints appeared which everyone thought to be the devil.
14. What activities were revealed by the presence of the strange footprints?
    The villagers' thievery, gluttony, and deceit were revealed wherever the footprints appeared.
15. Why was Will calling out from a pit to Alyce?
    His cow, Tansy, was about to deliver her calf and he needed help.
16. What did the villagers notice about Alyce in the late fall of that year?
    She grew in knowledge and skills and they began to ask her *how*, *why*, and *what can I?*
17. Why did Jane desert Joan, the bailiff's wife, during her labor?
    It was a difficult birth, one she assumed would end in stillbirth. Lady Agnes, at the manor, requested Jane, so she went to the manor to deliver Lady Agnes' baby and planned to return to take Joan's dead baby from her later and collect both fees.

18. How was Alyce able to help Joan along in her delivery?

    She gave her all she had of care, courtesy, and hard work.

19. How did Alyce react to her inability to deliver Emma's baby?

    She considered herself a failure and turned her back on all that she knew that had come to be dear to her and headed up the road from the village. The cat went with her.

20. What three offers does Alyce get that June from people she knows at the inn? What does Alyce decide she must do?

    Magister Reese wants her to return to Oxford with him to care for his widowed sister, the rich merchant and his wife want to take her back to Salisbury with them to care for their son, and Jennet offers her a raise to stay at the inn. She must return to the village and resume her midwife apprenticeship.

III. Essay

   When Alyce returns to Jane's she says she's changed. Will Alyce "try and risk and fail and try again? Support your answer.

   Answers will vary. Judge according to your own standards.

IV. Vocabulary

   Choose ten of the vocabulary words (found on pages 148-149) to read orally for the vocabulary section of the test.

ADVANCED SHORT ANSWER UNIT TEST - *The Midwife's Apprentice*

I. Matching

____ 1. PRETTY   A. How Will describes Alyce

____ 2. CAT   B. Jane Sharp christened Brat this

____ 3. RED   C. Will says Alyce has these

____ 4. GUTS   D. Will Russett's hair color

____ 5. MAGISTER REESE E. Beetle's only companion

____ 6. DUNG HEAP   F. Warm, rotting muck

____ 7. READ   G. Wife bore him a son delivered by Alyce at Inn

____ 8. FLASKS   H. What Alyce felt she did

____ 9. TANSY   I. Writer staying at Inn

____ 10. HERBS   J. Bartered for at the fair by Beetle

____ 11. ENCYCLOPAEDIA K. Will's mother cow

____ 12. BEETLE   L. Alyce learned to from Magister Reese

____ 13. PROSPEROUS MAN M. Used to treat mothers

____ 14. BRAT   N. Knew no home and no mother

____ 15. FAILED   O. Magister Reese's book

The Midwife's Apprentice Advanced Short Answer Unit Test Page 2

II. Short Answer

1. What does Alyce learn about herself from her experiences with the midwife?

2. Why do you think Alyce decided to save both the cat and Will, rather than let them die?

3. Who is responsible for Alyce's success and happiness? Defend your answer.

4. Is the story of *The Midwife's Apprentice* believable? Why or why not?

The Midwife's Apprentice Advanced Short Answer Unit Test Page 3

5. What universal themes appear in *The Midwife's Apprentice*? Explain.

6. Do you agree or disagree with Will who says, "Just because you don't know everything don't mean you know nothing." Support your opinion.

The Midwife's Apprentice Advanced Short Answer Unit Test Page 4

III. Quotations: Explain the importance and meaning of the following quotations.

1. "This face could belong to someone who can read. And has curls. And could have a lover before nightfall. And this is me."

2. "Touch that cat again and I will unstop this bottle of rat's blood and viper's flesh and summon the Devil, who will change you into women, and henceforth each of you will giggle like a woman and wear dresses like a woman and give birth like a woman!"

3. "We have no need of you, Jane. Your helper has taken care of us with her two strong hands and her good common sense."

4. "I am nothing, I have nothing, I can do nothing and learn nothing. I belong no place. I am too stupid to be a midwife's apprentice and too tired to wander again. I should just lie here in the rain until I die."

5. "I know what I want. A full belly, a contented heart, and a place in this world. This is what I want, but it is my misfortune instead to be hungry, out of humor, and too stupid to be a midwife's apprentice."

The Midwife's Apprentice Advanced Short Answer Unit Test Page 5

6. "And a prettier inn girl the world never saw, or you would be if you ever got that flour and dirt off yer face."

7. "Bah, Alyce. I seen you with Tansy. You got guts and common sense. Just because you don't know everything don't mean you know nothin'"

8. "Jane Sharp! It is I, Alyce, your apprentice. I have come back. And if you do not let me in, I will try again and again. I can do what you tell me and take what you give me, and I know how to try and risk and fail and try again and not give up. I will not go away."

The Midwife's Apprentice Advanced Short Answer Unit Test Page 6

IV. Vocabulary

Listen to the vocabulary words and write them down. After you have written down all the words, write a paragraph in which you use all the words. The paragraph must in some way relate to *The Midwife's Apprentice*.

MULTIPLE CHOICE UNIT TEST #1 - *The Midwife's Apprentice*

I. Matching

_____ 1. INN   A. Brat expected, dreamed, and hoped for this

_____ 2. ALYCE LITTLE   B. Water sold for remedy

_____ 3. JENNET DARK   C. Jane Sharp christened Brat this

_____ 4. BEETLE   D. Author

_____ 5. CLEAN   E. Baby that Alyce delivered

_____ 6. CUSHMAN   F. Bartered for at the fair by Beetle

_____ 7. SISTER   G. Tansy delivered these

_____ 8. TWINS   H. Manor folk thought Alyce was Edward's

_____ 9. MURDERER'S WASH I. Cat food

_____ 10. NOTHING   J. Jane Sharp's fingernails

_____ 11. READ   K. Ointment for mothers-to-be's aching legs

_____ 12. FLASKS   L. Where Alyce fled

_____ 13. SAINT SWITHIN'S M. Innkeeper's wife

_____ 14. CHEESE   N. Fair held at Goblet-Under-Green

_____ 15. GOOSE GREASE   O. Alyce learned to from Magister Reese

II. Multiple Choice

1. Brat was
    a. large-boned and pale.
    b. scrawny and underfed.
    c. twelve or thirteen years old.
    d. both b and c.

The Midwife's Apprentice Multiple Choice Unit Test 1 Page 2

2. Brat had a sunny outlook on her life.
    a. true
    b. false

3. Jane's new name for Beetle came from
    a. her former apprentice.
    b. where she found her.
    c. what she looked like.
    d. both b and c.

4. The town boys could be counted on to
    a. torment and tease Beetle and the cat.
    b. help Beetle out when she needed it.
    c. do odd jobs for Jane Sharp.
    d. play tag day in and out.

5. Which of the following was *not* one of Beetle's chores?
    a. washing the dishes.
    b. starting the fire.
    c. collecting the rain water.
    d. roasting the bacon.

6. Beetle began to learn midwifery by
    a. watching through the windows.
    b. peeking from a dark corner within the cottage.
    c. taking notes during the delivery.
    d. talking to the mothers after the births

7. The miller's wife was upset with Beetle because
    a. Jane was gone when she had promised to be there for her delivery.
    b. Beetle couldn't deliver her baby.
    c. Jane sent the wrong herbs.
    d. she brought the wrong basket for Jane.

8. What item did Beetle *not* acquire at the fair?
    a. murderer's wash water
    b. flasks
    c. a hairbrush
    d. nutmeg

The Midwife's Apprentice Multiple Choice Unit Test 1 Page 3

9. At the fair, Beetle was
    a. mistaken for someone who could read.
    b. winked at.
    c. given a gift.
    d. all of the above

10. Alyce helps Will Russet by
    a. sneaking food to him secretly.
    b. rescuing him from drowning.
    c. hiding him from the angry miller.
    d. defending him against the bullies.

11. Alyce became aware of how the villagers spent their time because
    a. she was sent to fetch and deliver messages at all times of day and night.
    b. she had no fear of the shadows.
    c. she learned how to listen well.
    d. she was observant when she helped deliver babies.

12. Select the one activity *not* discovered by following the strange footprints.
    a. the baker's unfaithfulness
    b. Jane Sharp's greediness
    c. Wat's gluttony
    d. the miller's thievery

13. After the baker's wife discovered her husband's folly, Alyce threw _____ into the river.
    a. herbs and salt
    b. one of Jane's concoctions
    c. blocks of wood carved in the shape of hooves
    d. some of the baker's rolls

14. When Alyce saw the town boys teasing the cat, she threw nuts at them and threatened them. How did they respond?
    a. They laughed at her.
    b. They threw nuts back at her.
    c. They were startled and unable to move.
    d. They held the cat hostage.

The Midwife's Apprentice Multiple Choice Unit Test 1 Page 4

15. Jane Sharp deserted Joan, the bailiff's wife, in her labor because
    a. Joan was uncooperative.
    b. Lady Agnes, at the manor, needed her at the same time.
    c. she assumed Joan's baby would be stillborn.
    d. both b and c

16. After Emma's baby's birth, Alyce
    a. feels like she has been successful once again.
    b. asks for Jane and Emma's forgiveness
    c. believes she is a nothing.
    d. cries aloud in sadness.

17. Alyce left Emma's cottage and went to
    a. the inn at the crossroads.
    b. the seaside.
    c. the dung heap.
    d. the manor where she had sent Edward hoping for a new job for herself.

18. Alyce is able to learn how to read and write at the inn.
    a. true
    b. false

19. Which of the following *doesn't* Alyce answer when asked by Magister Reese, "what do you want, inn girl?"
    a. a place in this world
    b. a contented heart
    c. a fully belly
    d. a yellow ribbon for my black hair

20. In order to get Jane Sharp to accept her back, Alyce had to promise to
    a. roast the snails better.
    b. try and risk and fail and try again.
    c. collect only the heaviest nuts and acorns.
    d. not steal her mothers way from her.

The Midwife's Apprentice Multiple Choice Unit Test 1 Page 5

III. Quotations: Identify the speaker:

A= Beetle   B= Jane Sharp   C= Will Russet   D= Jennet Dark

E= Magister Reese   F= Alyce   G= Edward

1. "Damn you, cat, breathe and live, you flea-bitten sod, or I'll kill you myself."

2. "Push, you cow. If an animal can do it, you can do it."

3. "And who would I be telling, then? I don't talk to no one but the cat and he don't care who you are kissin'."

4. "Broken by God's whiskers. Broken."

5. "Get out of my sight, Dung Beetle, before I squash you."

6. "Naw, I be not brave. I did it for else you'd have drowned and gone to Hell, a drunken loudmouth bully like you and I would have helped send you there and I could not have that, now, could I?"

7. "Touch that cat again and I will unstop this bottle of rat's blood and viper's flesh and summon the Devil, who will change you into women, and henceforth each of you will giggle like a woman and wear dresses like a woman and give birth like a woman!"

8. "Go then, such treachery! Such thievery! Eating my bread and stealing my mothers! Go!"

9. "This, puss, is my masterpiece, an encyclopaedic compendium I call the 'The Great Mirror of the Universe Wherein You Can Find Reflected All of the World's Knowledge, Collected by Myself and dedicated to His Ampleness the Bishop of Chester,' so called for he is ample in all the world's virtues."

10. "And what, inn girl, do *you* want?"

11. "I know what I want. A full belly, a contented heart, and a place in this world. This is what I want, but it is my misfortune instead to be hungry, out of humor, and too stupid to be a midwife's apprentice."

The Midwife's Apprentice Multiple Choice Unit Test 1 Page 6

12. "Thundering toads, I am but a poor woman with this wretched inn and a blind man to care for. I am sure God does not begrudge me my little economies."

13. "Bah, Alyce. I seen you with Tansy. You got guts and common sense. Just because you don't know everything don't mean you know nothin'"

14. "I need an apprentice who can do what I tell her, take what I give her, who can try and risk and fail and try again and not give up. Babies don't stop their borning because the midwife gives up."

15. "Not really lies, Alyce. I just wanted a sister, for all cook's other children have brothers and sisters. Have you come to take me away? You haven't, have you, Alyce? For I am sore content here and mostly have enough to eat, and when cook is cross with me I sleep with the chickens and pretend. No one chases me away and even Lord Arnulf knows my name. "

The Midwife's Apprentice Multiple Choice Unit Test 1 Page 7

IV. Vocabulary (Matching)

____ 1. BERATING   A. named

____ 2. TAUNTED   B. rich; fine

____ 3. PATERNOSTERS   C. energetic

____ 4. DESOLATE   D. turmoil

____ 5. REVELERS   E. dreadful; awful

____ 6. TUMULT   F. deserted; abandoned

____ 7. STOUT   G. beating grain to separate seeds from stalk

____ 8. VIGOROUS   H. parts of the Lord's prayer

____ 9. COMPENDIUM   I. effectiveness; capability

____ 10. HOIST   J. well-to-do

____ 11. RELUCTANT   K. many; numerous

____ 12. PROSPEROUS   L. scolding

____ 13. CHRISTENED   M. fascinatingly

____ 14. SUNDRY   N. heavy set

____ 15. MEWLING   O. drinkers; carousers

____ 16. TANTALIZINGLY   P. unwilling

____ 17. THRESHING   Q. whimpering; whining

____ 18. LUXURIOUS   R. mocked; sneered

____ 19. EFFICACY   S. comprehensive summary

____ 20. DIRE   T. lift up

MULTIPLE CHOICE UNIT TEST #2 - *The Midwife's Apprentice*

I. Matching

____ 1. COTTAGE FLOOR   A. Beetle's bed

____ 2. SAINT SWITHIN'S   B. Wife bore him a son delivered by Alyce at Inn

____ 3. MAGISTER REESE   C. Brat expected, dreamed, and hoped for this

____ 4. READ   D. Fair held at Goblet-Under-Green

____ 5. PROSPEROUS MAN   E. Magister Reese's book

____ 6. ANKLE   F. Broken when Jane tripped over pig

____ 7. FLASKS   G. Left mysterious footprints

____ 8. ALYCE LITTLE   H. Town boy Alyce saves

____ 9. NOTHING   I. Baby that Alyce delivered

____ 10. FIG   J. Writer staying at Inn

____ 11. ENCYCLOPAEDIA   K. Alyce learned to from Magister Reese

____ 12. HERBS   L. Babies Midwife bore and lost

____ 13. SIX   M. Bartered for at the fair by Beetle

____ 14. DEVIL   N. Used to treat mothers

____ 15. WILL RUSSET   O. Best tasting food to Edward

II. Multiple Choice
1. Jane Sharp appeared
        a. neither young nor old.
        b. neither fat not thin.
        c. important-looking.
        d. all of the above

The Midwife's Apprentice Multiple Choice Unit Test 2 Page 2

2. Jane's new name for Beetle came from
    a. her former apprentice.
    b. where she found her.
    c. what she looked like.
    d. both b and c.

3. The town boys could be counted on to
    a. torment and tease Beetle and the cat.
    b. help Beetle out when she needed it.
    c. do odd jobs for Jane Sharp.
    d. play tag day in and out

4. Jane Sharp was a generous and compassionate midwife.
    a. true
    b. false

5. At the fair, Beetle was
    a. mistaken for someone who could read.
    b. winked at.
    c. given a gift.
    d. all of the above

6. Alyce became aware of how the villagers spent their time because
    a. she was sent to fetch and deliver messages at all times of day and night.
    b. she had no fear of the shadows.
    c. she learned how to listen well.
    d. she was observant when she helped deliver babies.

7. When Alyce saw the town boys teasing the cat, she threw nuts at them and threatened them. How did they respond?
    a. The laughed at her.
    b. They threw nuts back at her.
    c. They were startled and unable to move.
    d. The held the cat hostage.

The Midwife's Apprentice Multiple Choice Unit Test 2 Page 3

8. Jane Sharp deserted Joan, the bailiff's wife, in her labor because
   a. Joan was uncooperative.
   b. Lady Agnes, at the manor, needed her at the same time.
   c. she assumed Joan's baby would be stillborn.
   d. both b and c

9. After delivering, Alyce Little, Joan, the bailiff's wife's baby, Alyce thought she knew most of what she needed to know about delivering babies.
   a. true
   b. false

10. When Alyce goes to visit Tansy's calves she finds
    a. Will crying because one of the calves died.
    b. that one of the calves has run off.
    c. Tansy has run off with the calves.
    d. a forlorn sleeping boy of about six years old.

11. Emma Blunt requested Alyce to deliver her baby because
    a. she had delivered her sister's baby.
    b. she was angry over Jane's greed.
    c. Alyce was highly regarded by all of the town.
    d. Alyce was a distant relative.

12. After Emma's baby's birth, Alyce
    a. feels like she has been successful once again.
    b. asks for Jane and Emma's forgiveness
    c. believes she is a nothing.
    d. cries aloud in sadness.

13. Alyce left Emma's cottage and went to
    a. the inn at the crossroads.
    b. the seaside.
    c. the dung heap.
    d. the manor where she had sent Edward hoping for a new job for herself.

The Midwife's Apprentice Multiple Choice Unit Test 2 Page 4

14. Which of the following *doesn't* Alyce answer when asked by Magister Reese, "what do you want, inn girl?"
    a. a place in this world
    b. a contented heart
    c. a fully belly
    d. a yellow ribbon for my black hair

15. Jane Sharp told Magister Reese that her former apprentice had failed.
    a. false
    b. true

16. When Alyce looks at her reflection in the river she
    a. is pleased.
    b. is disappointed
    c. is fearful.
    d. is confused.

17. The prosperous-looking inn visitor claims his wife
    a. has a stomach worm.
    b. is barren.
    c. has grown stout from too many potpies.
    d. Both a and b

18. Alyce gets involved in the visitors' situation by
    a. putting clean sheets on their bed.
    b. delivering their son.
    c. praying for the saints for the woman.
    d. offering to bring them ale and bread.

19. Who of the following does *not* make Alyce an offer that June?
    a. Jane Sharp
    b. Jennet Dark
    c. Magister Reese
    d. the rich merchant and his wife

20. Which of the following was *not* a mainstay of medieval midwifery?
    a. superstition
    b. common sense
    c. medical knowledge
    d. herbal knowledge

The Midwife's Apprentice Multiple Choice Unit Test 2 Page 5

III. Quotations: Identify the speaker:

A= Edward   B= Jennet Dark   C= Alyce   D= Jane Sharp

E= Beetle   F= Will Russet   G= Magister Reese

1. "Damn you, cat, breathe and live, you flea-bitten sod, or I'll kill you myself."

2. "Push, you cow. If an animal can do it, you can do it."

3. "And who would I be telling, then? I don't talk to no one but the cat and he don't care who you are kissin'."

4. "Broken by God's whiskers. Broken."

5. "Get out of my sight, Dung Beetle, before I squash you."

6. "Naw, I be not brave. I did it for else you'd have drowned and gone to Hell, a drunken loudmouth bully like you and I would have helped send you there and I could not have that, now, could I?"

7. "Touch that cat again and I will unstop this bottle of rat's blood and viper's flesh and summon the Devil, who will change you into women, and henceforth each of you will giggle like a woman and wear dresses like a woman and give birth like a woman!"

8. "Go then, such treachery! Such thievery! Eating my bread and stealing my mothers! Go!"

9. "This, puss, is my masterpiece, an encyclopaedic compendium I call the 'The Great Mirror of the Universe Wherein You Can Find Reflected All of the World's Knowledge, Collected by Myself and dedicated to His Ampleness the Bishop of Chester,' so called for he is ample in all the world's virtues."

10. "And what, inn girl, do *you* want?"

11. "I know what I want. A full belly, a contented heart, and a place in this world. This is what I want, but it is my misfortune instead to be hungry, out of humor, and too stupid to be a midwife's apprentice."

The Midwife's Apprentice Multiple Choice Unit Test 2 Page 6

12. "Thundering toads, I am but a poor woman with this wretched inn and a blind man to care for. I am sure God does not begrudge me my little economies."

13. "Bah, Alyce. I seen you with Tansy. You got guts and common sense. Just because you don't know everything don't mean you know nothin'"

14. "I need an apprentice who can do what I tell her, take what I give her, who can try and risk and fail and try again and not give up. Babies don't stop their borning because the midwife gives up."

15. "Not really lies, Alyce. I just wanted a sister, for all cook's other children have brothers and sisters. Have you come to take me away? You haven't, have you, Alyce? For I am sore content here and mostly have enough to eat, and when cook is cross with me I sleep with the chickens and pretend. No one chases me away and even Lord Arnulf knows my name."

The Midwife's Apprentice Multiple Choice Unit Test 2 page 7

IV. Vocabulary (Matching)

____ 1. VICTORIOUS   A. unmindful

____ 2. FERMENTING   B. dreadful; awful

____ 3. TAUNTED   C. effectiveness; capability

____ 4. BERATING   D. from now on

____ 5. HEEDLESS   E. an outhouse

____ 6. HENCEFORTH   F. successful

____ 7. EXERTIONS   G. deserted; abandoned

____ 8. MEWLING   H. bartering; dickering

____ 9. TWEAKED   I. excessive overeating

____ 10. DESOLATE   J. plenty

____ 11. BAILIFF   K. efforts; labors

____ 12. HAGGLING   L. ripening

____ 13. SOOTHSAYERS   M. stupidity; inability

____ 14. ABUNDANCE   N. whimpering; whining

____ 15. WRITHING   O. turning and twisting from pain

____ 16. INCOMPETENCE   P. prophets; fortunetellers

____ 17. GLUTTONY   Q. arresting officer

____ 18. PRIVY   R. scolding

____ 19. EFFICACY   S. mocked; sneered

____ 20. DIRE   T. a sharp pull or twist

ANSWER SHEET - *The Midwife's Apprentice*
Multiple Choice Unit Tests

I. Matching
1. ___
2. ___
3. ___
4. ___
5. ___
6. ___
7. ___
8. ___
9. ___
10. ___
11. ___
12. ___
13. ___
14. ___
15. ___

II. Quotes
1. (A) (B) (C) (D) (E) (F) (G)
2. (A) (B) (C) (D) (E) (F) (G)
3. (A) (B) (C) (D) (E) (F) (G)
4. (A) (B) (C) (D) (E) (F) (G)
5. (A) (B) (C) (D) (E) (F) (G)
6. (A) (B) (C) (D) (E) (F) (G)
7. (A) (B) (C) (D) (E) (F) (G)
8. (A) (B) (C) (D) (E) (F) (G)
9. (A) (B) (C) (D) (E) (F) (G)
10. (A) (B) (C) (D) (E) (F) (G)
11. (A) (B) (C) (D) (E) (F) (G)
12. (A) (B) (C) (D) (E) (F) (G)
13. (A) (B) (C) (D) (E) (F) (G)
14. (A) (B) (C) (D) (E) (F) (G)
15. (A) (B) (C) (D) (E) (F) (G)

II. Multiple Choice
1. (A) (B) (C) (D)
2. (A) (B) (C) (D)
3. (A) (B) (C) (D)
4. (A) (B) (C) (D)
5. (A) (B) (C) (D)
6. (A) (B) (C) (D)
7. (A) (B) (C) (D)
8. (A) (B) (C) (D)
9. (A) (B) (C) (D)
10. (A) (B) (C) (D)
11. (A) (B) (C) (D)
12. (A) (B) (C) (D)
13. (A) (B) (C) (D)
14. (A) (B) (C) (D)
15. (A) (B) (C) (D)
16. (A) (B) (C) (D)
17. (A) (B) (C) (D)
18. (A) (B) (C) (D)
19. (A) (B) (C) (D)
20. (A) (B) (C) (D)

V. Vocabulary
1. ___
2. ___
3. ___
4. ___
5. ___
6. ___
7. ___
8. ___
9. ___
10. ___
11. ___
12. ___
13. ___
14. ___
15. ___
16. ___
17. ___
18. ___
19. ___
20. ___

ANSWER SHEET KEY - *The Midwife's Apprentice*
Multiple Choice Unit Test 1

I. Matching
1. L
2. E
3. M
4. C
5. J
6. D
7. H
8. G
9. B
10. A
11. O
12. F
13. N
14. I
15. K

II. Quotes
1. ( ) (B) (C) (D) (E) (F) (G)
2. (A) ( ) (C) (D) (E) (F) (G)
3. ( ) (B) (C) (D) (E) (F) (G)
4. (A) ( ) (C) (D) (E) (F) (G)
5. (A) ( ) (C) (D) (E) (F) (G)
6. (A) (B) (C) (D) (E) ( ) (G)
7. (A) (B) (C) (D) (E) ( ) (G)
8. (A) ( ) (C) (D) (E) (F) (G)
9. (A) (B) (C) (D) ( ) (F) (G)
10. (A) (B) (C) (D) ( ) (F) (G)
11. (A) (B) (C) (D) (E) ( ) (G)
12. (A) (B) (C) ( ) (E) (F) (G)
13. (A) (B) ( ) (D) (E) (F) (G)
14. (A) ( ) (C) (D) (E) (F) (G)
15. (A) (B) (C) (D) (E) (F) ( )

II. Multiple Choice
1. (A) (B) (C) ( )
2. (A) ( ) (C) (D)
3. (A) (B) (C) ( )
4. ( ) (B) (C) (D)
5. (A) (B) ( ) (D)
6. ( ) (B) (C) (D)
7. (A) ( ) (C) (D)
8. (A) (B) ( ) (D)
9. (A) (B) (C) ( )
10. (A) ( ) (C) (D)
11. ( ) (B) (C) (D)
12. (A) ( ) (C) (D)
13. (A) (B) ( ) (D)
14. (A) (B) ( ) (D)
15. (A) (B) (C) ( )
16. (A) (B) ( ) (D)
17. ( ) (B) (C) (D)
18. ( ) (B) (C) (D)
19. (A) (B) (C) ( )
20. (A) ( ) (C) (D)

V. Vocabulary
1. L
2. R
3. H
4. F
5. O
6. D
7. N
8. C
9. S
10. T
11. P
12. J
13. A
14. K
15. Q
16. M
17. G
18. B
19. I
20. E

ANSWER SHEET KEY - *The Midwife's Apprentice*
Multiple Choice Unit Test 2

I. Matching
1. A
2. D
3. J
4. K
5. B
6. F
7. M
8. I
9. C
10. O
11. E
12. N
13. L
14. G
15. H

II. Multiple Choice
1. (A) (B) (C) ( )
2. (A) (B) (C) ( )
3. ( ) (B) (C) (D)
4. (A) ( ) (C) (D)
5. (A) (B) (C) ( )
6. ( ) (B) (C) (D)
7. (A) (B) ( ) (D)
8. (A) (B) (C) ( )
9. (A) ( ) (C) (D)
10. (A) (B) (C) ( )
11. ( ) (B) (C) (D)
12. (A) (B) ( ) (D)
13. ( ) (B) (C) (D)
14. (A) (B) (C) ( )
15. ( ) (B) (C) (D)
16. ( ) (B) (C) (D)
17. (A) (B) (C) ( )
18. (A) ( ) (C) (D)
19. ( ) (B) (C) (D)
20. (A) (B) ( ) (D)

II. Quotes
1. (A) (B) (C) (D) ( ) (F) (G)
2. (A) (B) (C) ( ) (E) (F) (G)
3. (A) (B) (C) (D) ( ) (F) (G)
4. (A) (B) (C) ( ) (E) (F) (G)
5. (A) (B) (C) ( ) (E) (F) (G)
6. (A) (B) ( ) (D) (E) (F) (G)
7. (A) (B) ( ) (D) (E) (F) (G)
8. (A) (B) (C) ( ) (E) (F) (G)
9. (A) (B) (C) (D) (E) (F) ( )
10. (A) (B) (C) (D) (E) (F) ( )
11. (A) (B) ( ) (D) (E) (F) (G)
12. (A) ( ) (C) (D) (E) (F) (G)
13. (A) (B) (C) (D) (E) ( ) (G)
14. (A) (B) (C) ( ) (E) (F) (G)
15. ( ) (B) (C) (D) (E) (F) (G)

V. Vocabulary
1. F
2. L
3. S
4. R
5. A
6. D
7. K
8. N
9. T
10. G
11. Q
12. H
13. P
14. J
15. O
16. M
17. I
18. E
19. C
20. B

UNIT RESOURCE MATERIALS

BULLETIN BOARD IDEAS - *The Midwife's Apprentice*

1. Post students' Writing Assignment #1, Missing Posters, appealing for Alyce's return.

2. Bring in (or have students bring in) pictures of babies, Medieval England, cows, calves, Renaissance Fairs, herbs, cats, English country villages, inns, sheep, etc. Make a collage if you have enough different pictures (or post individual pictures on colorful paper if you only have a few pictures). This could also be a fun introductory activity if students participate. You could have the border and title " A Journey Home" done for the bulletin board and invite students to staple up their own pictures wherever they want them. It will only take a few minutes of class time, but the students will enjoy it and you can get your bulletin board done in a hurry.

3. Draw one of the word search puzzles onto the bulletin board. (Be sure to enlarge it.) Write the key words to one side. Invite students to take their pens or markers and find the words before and/or after class (or perhaps this could be an activity for students who finish their work early).

4. Create a display of perfectly formed alphabet letters like Alyce was learning from Magister Reese at the inn.

5. Have students generate their impression of the treasured wooden cat comb Beetle was given at the Saint Swithin's Day Fair.

6. Illustrate the main characters by either silhouettes, portraits, or whatever your choice. Include information gained from the novel describing them.

7. Post the words to the song by Alyce about Tansy's birth of twins. Have students illustrate according to their interpretation of the poem.

8. Make a mural depicting the village and the surrounding areas. Be sure to include the inn and the manor.

9. Post any of the students' Writing Assignments, in addition to their Missing Posters. They could illustrate something from their Writing Assignment to enhance it.

10. Create a collage of art work from students that conveys their impressions of the characters in this story.

11. Post pictures of herbs and their scientific names and uses.

12. Portray Brat, Beetle, and Alyce. Even though they are all the same young lady, she probably looked different at the different stages of her journey to self-awareness.

EXTRA ACTIVITIES - *The Midwife's Apprentice*

One of the difficulties in teaching a novel is that all students don't read at the same speed. One student who likes to read may take the book home and finish it in a day or two. Sometimes a few students finish the in-class assignments early. The problem, then, is finding suitable extra activities for students.

One thing you can do is to keep a little library in the classroom. For this unit on *The Midwife's Apprentice*, you might check out from the school library other books by Karen Cushman. A biography of the author would be interesting for some students. Books on Medieval England, midwifery, babies, herbs, superstitions, Renaissance Fairs, etc. might prove useful.

Other things you may keep on hand are puzzles. We have made some relating directly to *The Midwife's Apprentice* for you. Feel free to duplicate them.

Some students may like to draw. You might devise a contest or allow some extra-credit grade for students who draw characters or scenes from *The Midwife's Apprentice*. Note, too, that if the students do not want to keep their drawings you may pick up some extra bulletin board materials this way. You could have a contest and supply a prize or, you could possibly make the drawing itself a non-refundable entry fee.

The pages which follow contain games, puzzles and worksheets. The keys, when appropriate, immediately follow the puzzle or worksheet. There are two main groups of activities: one group for the unit; that is, generally relating to *The Midwife's Apprentice* text, and another group of activities related strictly to *The Midwife's Apprentice* vocabulary.

Directions for the games, puzzles and worksheets are self-explanatory. The object here is to provide you with extra materials you may use in any way you choose.

MORE ACTIVITIES - *The Midwife's Apprentice*

1. Pick a chapter or scene with a great deal of dialogue and have the students act it out on a stage. (Perhaps you could assign various scenes to different groups of students so more than one scene could be acted and more students could participate.)

2. Listen to the audio tape version of this novel. Have the students evaluate the voices used on the tape. Do they match what they imagined the characters would sound like as they read the book?

3. Have students design a book cover (front and back and inside flaps) for *The Midwife's Apprentice*.

4. Students could write a sequel chapter that explains how Alyce gets along now with Jane. Does she ultimately become a full-fledged midwife?

5. Debate the advantages or disadvantages of using a midwife for a delivery as compared to a traditional medical doctor and a hospital setting.

6. Use some of the related topics (noted earlier for an in-class library) as topics for research, reports or written papers, or as topics for guest speakers.

7. Have students plan and teach a lesson on a chapter or section of the book. Give them guidelines and a time frame.

8. Visit a maternity ward, if possible and discover the mothers' feelings about caring for their babies and their apprehensions.

9. Have an animal naming contest. Adopt a class pet or mascot (even if just a picture) and hold a contest to name it.

10. Write to Karen Cushman asking her questions students have composed. You could send a class set of letters in one large envelope.

11. Construct models of the various places mentioned in the setting. Put together into a diorama or a large scale model of the village and surrounding areas.

12. Research music, fashions, hairstyles, activities, etc. of this era and geography. Present to the class through a skit or play.

13. Create a pet-owner chart. Have students bring in pictures of their pets and post. Discuss the value of owning pets and how Purr helped Alyce throughout the story.

More Activities - *The Midwife's Apprentice* Page 2

14. Invite a willing relative of your students in to share information about the main topic with the class. Maybe a class member could bring in a very young sibling and the parent could share appropriate information about the birth or delivery.

15. Have students interview someone who has used a midwife for a delivery, if possible. Have students compose questions together for their interviews. They could then make a booklet with the information in it for display. Have them illustrate the cover with something they learned about the topic from their interview.

16. Allow students to select a character from the novel. Have them dress like them, speak like them; assume their persona. Create a talk show format with these characters as the guests. Have a student volunteer to be the host. Others not involved will be the audience, questioning the characters. One of your students could pretend to be a trained psychologist who comes out later in the show to help the panel solve their problems. Have a topic like: lack of self-esteem, inferiority, i.e. problems encountered in the novel. Allow the class to decide as much as possible. Have questions from the audience ready prior to the show day. You could have students try out for the parts. Remind them to keep it on the up and up, not to mimic some of the seedier talk shows. This will require students to take an in-depth look into characterization in the novel.

17. View a filmstrip or a video on Karen Cushman, if available.

18. Students who like board games may want to create one using information from this novel. Some students could work together as a group to complete this task. Encourage them to look at setting to illustrate their board and possibly use vocabulary, characters, plot, etc. for question cards.

19. Write and sing some simple songs like Alyce wrote. Discuss the importance of music to good feelings. Share some of the class' favorite music and how it makes them feel.

20. Visit a midwife's office or a birthing center. Visit a traditional maternity ward at a hospital. Compare them.

21. Discuss ways to handle feelings of inferiority, such as Beetle's. Discuss what contributed to the ultimate elimination of this self-destructive feeling.

22. Invite a midwife to address key issues inherent to this story.

23. Review many of the herbs and concoctions mentioned in the book that were used for treatment of the mothers or babies. Research their effectiveness. Perhaps prepare some of them and share with the class.

More Activities - *The Midwife's Apprentice* Page 3

24. Hold a debate on the issue of Jane's manner with Alyce and with her mothers.

25. Create a compilation of different doctors' or nurses' styles. Discuss how different styles affect the patients. Should all medical practitioners share a common approach? Why or why not?

WORD SEARCH 1 - *The Midwife's Apprentice*

All words in this list are associated with The Midwife's Apprentice. The words are placed backwards, forward, diagonally, up and down. The clues below the word search can help you find the words.

```
R L E Z L P R E T T Y U S O R I C A R I I A U L
R J A G T A Q K X F B R J I O N A N O S D N N Y
R E D G U T S E D W A R D N X D T S M T W O G X
L N C G O J A K F T K I A M B O C Y M E I R H C
H N J W L B I H S J E C L T Z W G A E R F F E F
B E F U D X N V J V R A U E B S R N T S E H A T
E T W I N S T C O R I B L S D R E B T C H Y P V
E T H E O O S L H C N L R Y H Z E V S P O E B V
T D D M R X W E N E N H L E C M D R M C H M E D
L A H M T S I A D D E S E A A E A X I Y K D B P
E R O A H X T N A Q E S L R G D L N T S F I G Y
T K O B R R H Q R L L V E A B E G I H M K A A P
G L V L O T I P K T Y H I Z P S B Y T Y Q N V X
Q R E U A V N V N V B C F L G P M O H T F K E W
R G S N D R ' F B V F D E R D P E K Y Z L L U Z
P S P T X L S S F N O T H I N G T D D S P E P Q
```

ALYCE	EDWARD	JENNET DARK	SHEEP
ALYCE LITTLE	EEL	JOHN DARK	SISTER
ANKLE	EMMA BLUNT	JUNO	SIX
BAKER	FAILED	MANOR	SLAPPED
BEETLE	FIG	MIDWIFE	TANSY
BRAT	FLASKS	NOTHING	TWINS
BREAD	GAVE UP	OLD NORTH ROAD	TWO
CAT	GREED	PRETTY	VILLAGE BOYS
CHEESE	GROMMET SMITH	PURR	WINDOWS
CLEAN	GUTS	READ	WOOD CAT COMB
CUSHMAN	HERBS	RED	
DEVIL	HOOVES	RISK	
DUNG HEAP	INN	SAINT SWITHIN'	

KEY: WORD SEARCH - *The Midwife's Apprentice*

All the words in this list are associated with *The Midwife's Apprentice*. The words are placed backwards, forward, diagonally, up and down. The included words are listed below the word search.

```
            R F           P W     W   T G S M M D
            E  L P R E T T Y U S O   I C A R I I A U
      J  A     A        F B R   I O N A N O S D N N
   R E D G U T S E D W A R D   X D T S M T W O G
      N   O   A K     K I A     O C Y M E I R H
      N J   L   I   S   E C L T   W G A E R F   E
   B E   U D   N   J V R A U E     S R   T S E   A
   E T W I N S T C O   I B L S D   E   T C H   P
   E T   E O O S L H   N L R Y H   E   S   O E
   T D   M R   W E N E N H L E C M D R M     M E
   L A H M T   I A D D E S E A A E A   I     B P
   E R O A H   T N A   E S L R G D L N T S F I G
      K O B R   H   R L L V E A B E   I H   K A A
         V L O   I   K   Y   I   P S B   T     N V
         E U A   N       C   L   P   O   T   K E
         S N D   '       E       E   Y   L L U
            T   S     N O T H I N G   D   S   E P
```

ALYCE	EDWARD	JENNET DARK	SHEEP
ALYCE LITTLE	EEL	JOHN DARK	SISTER
ANKLE	EMMA BLUNT	JUNO	SIX
BAKER	FAILED	MANOR	SLAPPED
BEETLE	FIG	MIDWIFE	TANSY
BRAT	FLASKS	NOTHING	TWINS
BREAD	GAVE UP	OLD NORTH ROAD	TWO
CAT	GREED	PRETTY	VILLAGE BOYS
CHEESE	GROMMET SMITH	PURR	WINDOWS
CLEAN	GUTS	READ	WOOD CAT COMB
CUSHMAN	HERBS	RED	
DEVIL	HOOVES	RISK	
DUNG HEAP	INN	SAINT SWITHIN'S	

CROSSWORD - *The Midwife's Apprentice*

CROSSWORD CLUES - *The Midwife's Apprentice*

ACROSS
2. Ointment for mothers-to-be's aching legs; ___ grease
5. Father of thirteen children
7. Beetle longed to own it; wood cat ____
8. New name for cat
9. Left mysterious footprints
11. Alyce learned to from Magister Reese
12. Animals Alyce helped to scrub
16. Warm, rotting muck
18. Beetle watched through these and learned trade
22. Meals a day for Beetle
23. Bartered for at the fair by Beetle
26. Will's mother cow
28. Tormented Beetle; village ____
29. Beetle's only companion
30. Where Alyce fled
32. Knew no home and no mother
34. How Will describes Alyce
35. Jane Sharp's fingernails
37. Roman goddess of moon, women, and childbirth
38. Smith's lardy daughter; ___ Smith
42. Fair held at Goblet-Under-Green; Saint ____'s
44. Writer staying at Inn; Magister ____
45. Where Alyce sent Edward
46. Midwife's claim of what Alyce did
47. Innkeeper; ____ Dark

DOWN
1. Assistant
2. Midwife's fault
3. Babies Midwife bore and lost
4. Town boy Alyce saves; Russet
5. Gifts from baker to Jane
6. Alyce feared taking this
7. Cat food
10. Mother's whose baby Alyce failed to deliver; ___ Bluntc
13. Alyce's desire for her life; ___ in this world
14. Broken when Jane tripped over pig
15. Best tasting food to Edward____
17. Cat's rival in burlap sack in pond
19. Where Beetle found Jane and the baker kissing; ___ Road
20. Manor folk thought Alyce was____ Edward's
21. Brat expected, dreamed, and hoped for this
23. Beetle's bed; cottage
24. How Jane settled down the miller's wife
25. Magister Reese's book
27. Tansy delivered these
31. Will Russett's hair color
32. Jane Sharp christened Brat this
33. Name for someone who looked like they could read
33. Baby that Alyce delivered; _____ Little
36. Alyce sent him to the manor to do threshing
37. Innkeeper's wife; ____ Dark
38. Will says Alyce has these
39. Threw things at Beetle for her incompetence; ____'s wife
40. Author
43. Used to treat mothers

CROSSWORD ANSWER KEY - *The Midwife's Apprentice*

MATCHING QUIZ/WORKSHEET 1 - *The Midwife's Apprentice*

____ 1. CUSHMAN   A. Wooden prints carved by Alyce

____ 2. JENNET DARK   B. Woman who delivers babies

____ 3. EDWARD   C. Ointment for mothers-to-be's aching legs

____ 4. TWINS   D. Water sold for remedy

____ 5. GROMMET SMITH   E. Where Beetle found Jane and the baker kissing

____ 6. WOODEN CAT COMB   F. Alyce sent him to the manor to do threshing

____ 7. WINDOWS   G. Where Alyce sent Edward

____ 8. HERBS   H. Beetle's bed

____ 9. TWO   I. Beetle longed to own it

____ 10. SIX   J. Midwife's claim of what Alyce did

____ 11. GUTS   K. Babies Midwife bore and lost

____ 12. GOOSE GREASE   L. Author

____ 13. MIDWIFE   M. Used to treat mothers

____ 14. MANOR   N. Smith's lardy daughter

____ 15. OLD NORTH ROAD   O. Beetle watched through these and learned trade

____ 16. HOOVES   P. Innkeeper's wife

____ 17. GAVE UP   Q. Midwife's fault

____ 18. GREED   R. Tansy delivered these

____ 19. COTTAGE FLOOR   S. Will says Alyce has these

____ 20. MURDERER'S WASH T. Meals a day for Beetle

KEY: MATCHING QUIZ/WORKSHEET 1 - *The Midwife's Apprentice*

L - 1. CUSHMAN   A. Wooden prints carved by Alyce

P - 2. JENNET DARK   B. Woman who delivers babies

F - 3. EDWARD   C. Ointment for mothers-to-be's aching legs

R - 4. TWINS   D. Water sold for remedy

N - 5. GROMMET SMITH   E. Where Beetle found Jane and the baker kissing

I - 6. WOODEN CAT COMB   F. Alyce sent him to the manor to do threshing

O - 7. WINDOWS   G. Where Alyce sent Edward

M - 8. HERBS   H. Beetle's bed

T - 9. TWO   I. Beetle longed to own it

K - 10. SIX   J. Midwife's claim of what Alyce did

S - 11. GUTS   K. Babies Midwife bore and lost

C - 12. GOOSE GREASE   L. Author

B - 13. MIDWIFE   M. Used to treat mothers

G - 14. MANOR   N. Smith's lardy daughter

E - 15. OLD NORTH ROAD   O. Beetle watched through these and learned trade

A - 16. HOOVES   P. Innkeeper's wife

J - 17. GAVE UP   Q. Midwife's fault

Q - 18. GREED   R. Tansy delivered these

H - 19. COTTAGE FLOOR   S. Will says Alyce has these

D - 20. MURDERER'S WASH T. Meals a day for Beetle

MATCHING QUIZ/WORKSHEET 2 - *The Midwife's Apprentice*

____ 1. ALYCE LITTLE   A. Baby that Alyce delivered

____ 2. TWO   B. Beetle's bed

____ 3. FLASKS   C. How Will describes Alyce

____ 4. BREAD   D. Cat food

____ 5. GREED   E. Broken when Jane tripped over pig

____ 6. EMMA BLUNT   F. Roman goddess of moon, women, and childbirth

____ 7. CAT   G. Midwife's fault

____ 8. JUNO   H. Brat expected, dreamed, and hoped for this

____ 9. JENNET DARK   I. Mother's whose baby Alyce failed to deliver

____ 10. PRETTY   J. Gifts from baker to Jane

____ 11. EEL   K. Writer staying at Inn

____ 12. ENCYCLOPAEDIA   L. Beetle's only companion

____ 13. NOTHING   M. Cat's rival in burlap sack in pond

____ 14. GAVE UP   N. Magister Reese's book

____ 15. COTTAGE FLOOR   O. Beetle watched through these and learned trade

____ 16. WINDOWS   P. Meals a day for Beetle

____ 17. GROMMET SMITH   Q. Innkeeper's wife

____ 18. CHEESE   R. Midwife's claim of what Alyce did

____ 19. MAGISTER REESE   S. Smith's lardy daughter

____ 20. ANKLE   T. Bartered for at the fair by Beetle

KEY: MATCHING QUIZ/WORKSHEET 2 - *The Midwife's Apprentice*

A - 1. ALYCE LITTLE   A. Baby that Alyce delivered

P - 2. TWO   B. Beetle's bed

T - 3. FLASKS   C. How Will describes Alyce

J - 4. BREAD   D. Cat food

G - 5. GREED   E. Broken when Jane tripped over pig

I - 6. EMMA BLUNT   F. Roman goddess of moon, women, and childbirth

L - 7. CAT   G. Midwife's fault

F - 8. JUNO   H. Brat expected, dreamed, and hoped for this

Q - 9. JENNET DARK   I. Mother's whose baby Alyce failed to deliver

C - 10. PRETTY   J. Gifts from baker to Jane

M - 11. EEL   K. Writer staying at Inn

N - 12. ENCYCLOPAEDIA   L. Beetle's only companion

H - 13. NOTHING   M. Cat's rival in burlap sack in pond

R - 14. GAVE UP   N. Magister Reese's book

B - 15. COTTAGE FLOOR   O. Beetle watched through these and learned trade

O - 16. WINDOWS   P. Meals a day for Beetle

S - 17. GROMMET SMITH   Q. Innkeeper's wife

D - 18. CHEESE   R. Midwife's claim of what Alyce did

K - 19. MAGISTER REESE   S. Smith's lardy daughter

E - 20. ANKLE   T. Bartered for at the fair by Beetle

JUGGLE LETTER REVIEW GAME CLUE SHEET - *The Midwife's Apprentice*

SCRAMBLED	WORD	CLUE
NNI	INN	Where Alyce fled
OSVEHO	HOOVES	Wooden prints carved by Alyce
RATB	BRAT	Knew no home and no mother
RTIESS	SISTER	Manor folk thought Alyce was Edward's
LEE	EEL	Cat's rival in burlap sack in pond
EPECPIRTAN	APPRENTICE	Assistant
UTSG	GUTS	Will says Alyce has these
ILTLCYEETLA	ALYCE LITTLE	Baby that Alyce delivered
OWTBOMCEACDNO	WOODEN CAT COMB	Beetle longed to own it
UANSHMC	CUSHMAN	Author
ONUJ	JUNO	Roman goddess of moon, women, and childbirth
NNATWIHSSIT'IS	SAINT SWITHIN'S	Fair held at Goblet-Under-Green
SAPRUMPSEOONR	PROSPEROUS MAN	Wife bore him a son delivered by Alyce at Inn
IIHSNEWDTLCLROPA	PLACE IN THIS WORLD	Alyce's desire for her life
EPESH	SHEEP	Animals Alyce helped to scrub
SKRI	RISK	Alyce feared taking this
DARE	READ	Alyce learned to from Magister Reese
APENDHUG	DUNG HEAP	Warm, rotting muck
OSAESEERGOG	GOOSE GREASE	Ointment for mothers-to-be's aching legs
NHDKOJAR	JOHN DARK	Innkeeper
UPEAVG	GAVE UP	Midwife's claim of what Alyce did
ANORM	MANOR	Where Alyce sent Edward
TBUMNEAML	EMMA BLUNT	Mother's whose baby Alyce failed to deliver
OTOFTRGOCAEL	COTTAGE FLOOR	Beetle's bed
EDR	RED	Will Russet's hair color
REEDG	GREED	Midwife's fault
XSI	SIX	Babies Midwife bore and lost
DFLIAE	FAILED	What Alyce felt she did
WISTN	TWINS	Tansy delivered these
RRUP	PURR	New name for cat
GFI	FIG	Best tasting food to Edward
LTEBEE	BEETLE	Jane Sharp christened Brat this
RHOOLORDDATN	OLD NORTH ROAD	Where Beetle found Jane and the baker kissing
DOWISWN	WINDOWS	Beetle watched through these and learned trade
IGNOHTN	NOTHING	Brat expected, dreamed, and hoped for this

VOCABULARY RESOURCE MATERIALS

VOCABULARY WORD SEARCH - *The Midwife's Apprentice*

All the words in this list are associated with *The Midwife's Apprentice* with emphasis on the vocabulary words being studied in the unit. The words are placed backwards, forward, diagonally, up and down. The clues below the word search will help identify the words used.

```
R H W P N S O L E M N I T Y I G N O R A N C E K
E E F R J O U S U F E R N W X Z R D S B I O M H
P E T I H O V N T X F A E N E Y H Y H B M M E L
L D G V L T T I D U U I N S O A R A X E B P W M
E L I Y M H U A C R P R C D I V K E G Y L E L P
N E S R M S M S U T Y E I A E S A E A G E N I F
I S T Y E A U H W N O J F O C R T T D S L D N P
S S O J S Y L X E B T R K I U Y E A I K S I G X
H V U Q U E T F X N D E I Q E S Q D N O R U N W
R X T P L R G K E H C V D O L D K B L C N M R G
D E S O L A T E R O R E S O U N D E D B E W B E
L E N D E U B H T I Y L F P M S W R F A X I L Y
N C C O N F C Y I S Y E K O W T F A K I S M I W
L B Z E W D M K O T Y R Q L R G G T H L P P G R
V D L F I N Y R N V Q S T S S T B I K I D L H X
X K J N F T E X S W R H H Q C N H N H F M E T Y
Y R T A B U N D A N C E S X H J Q G Z F Z B J M
```

ABBEY	EXERTIONS	NIMBLE	SOOTHSAYER
ABUNDANCE	HAGGLING	PLUCK	STOUT
BAILIFF	HEEDLESS	PRIVY	STUPEFIED
BERATING	HENCEFORTH	REASSURE	SULLEN
BLIGHT	HOIST	RENOWNED	SUNDRY
COMPENDIUM	IGNORANCE	REPLENISH	TAUNTED
DECEIT	INNOVATION	RESISTANCE	TUMULT
DESOLATE	LUXURIOUS	RESOUNDED	TWEAKED
DIRE	MEANDERED	REVELERS	VICTORIOUS
EFFICACY	MEWLING	SOLEMNITY	WIMPLE

KEY: VOCABULARY WORD SEARCH - *The Midwife's Apprentice*

All the words in this list are associated with *The Midwife's Apprentice* with emphasis on the vocabulary words being studied in the unit. The words are placed backwards, forward, diagonally, up and down.

```
R H   P   S O L E M N I T Y I G N O R A N C E
E E   R   O U S U F E R N W       B I O M
P E   I   O V N T X F A E N E   H   B M M E
L D   V   T T I D U U I N S O A R A   E B P W
E L I Y   H U A C R P R C D I V K E G Y L E L
N E S R   S M   U T Y E I A E S A E A G E N I
I S T   E A U H   N O   F O C R T T D S L D N
S S O   S Y L   E   T R   I U Y E A I   S I G
H   U   U E T   X N   E I   E S   D N O   U N
R   T P L R     E H C V D O   D   B   C N M R G
D E S O L A T E R O R E S O U N D E D B E W B E
  E N   E U   T I   L F     S   R   A   I L
    C O N   C   I S   E   O       A   I   M I
      E W     K O T   R       R     T L   P G
        I N     N     S           T   I I   L H
          T E   S                   H   N   F   E T
        A B U N D A N C E             G   F
```

ABBEY	EXERTIONS	NIMBLE	SOOTHSAYER
ABUNDANCE	HAGGLING	PLUCK	STOUT
BAILIFF	HEEDLESS	PRIVY	STUPEFIED
BERATING	HENCEFORTH	REASSURE	SULLEN
BLIGHT	HOIST	RENOWNED	SUNDRY
COMPENDIUM	IGNORANCE	REPLENISH	TAUNTED
DECEIT	INNOVATION	RESISTANCE	TUMULT
DESOLATE	LUXURIOUS	RESOUNDED	TWEAKED
DIRE	MEANDERED	REVELERS	VICTORIOUS
EFFICACY	MEWLING	SOLEMNITY	WIMPLE

VOCABULARY CROSSWORD - *The Midwife's Apprentice*

VOCABULARY CROSSWORD CLUES - *Midwife's Apprentice*

ACROSS
1. dreadful; awful
3. stopping the flow
10. silent
12. ripening
14. comprehensive summary
16. named
19. woman's headcloth drawn in folds about the chin
23. whimpering; whining
24. restock
28. turmoil
29. heavy set
30. efforts; labors

DOWN
1. dishonesty
2. opposition
3. many; numerous
4. convent; monastery
5. unmindful
6. lively; quick
7. arresting officer
8. stupidity; inability
9. unawareness; inexperience
11. rich; fine
13. spirit; spunk
15. rambled
16. sympathy; caring
17. unwilling
18. mocked; sneered
19. turning and twisting from pain
20. seriousness
21. uninhabited islands S.E. of New Zealand
22. energetic
25. bartering; dickering
26. lift up
27. curse

VOCABULARY CROSSWORD ANSWER KEY - *The Midwife's Apprentice*

VOCABULARY WORKSHEET 1 - *The Midwife's Apprentice*

____ 1. PLUCK   A. a sharp pull or twist

____ 2. INNOVATION   B. unmindful

____ 3. LUXURIOUS   C. unawareness; inexperience

____ 4. BERATING   D. an improvement

____ 5. TWEAKED   E. stopping the flow

____ 6. IGNORANCE   F. fascinatingly

____ 7. RESISTANCE   G. stupidity; inability

____ 8. INCOMPETENCE   H. whimpering; whining

____ 9. REPLENISH   I. spirit; spunk

____ 10. NIMBLE   J. restock

____ 11. EFFICACY   K. dreadful; awful

____ 12. DESOLATE   L. sympathy; caring

____ 13. RELUCTANT   M. lively; quick

____ 14. MEWLING   N. scolding

____ 15. SOLEMNITY   O. rich; fine

____ 16. COMPASSION   P. effectiveness; capability

____ 17. HEEDLESS   Q. deserted; abandoned

____ 18. STANCHING   R. opposition

____ 19. DIRE   S. seriousness

____ 20. TANTALIZINGLY   T. unwilling

KEY: VOCABULARY WORKSHEET 1 - *The Midwife's Apprentice*

I - 1. PLUCK		A. a sharp pull or twist
D - 2. INNOVATION		B. unmindful
O - 3. LUXURIOUS		C. unawareness; inexperience
N - 4. BERATING		D. an improvement
A - 5. TWEAKED		E. stopping the flow
C - 6. IGNORANCE		F. fascinatingly
R - 7. RESISTANCE		G. stupidity; inability
G - 8. INCOMPETENCE		H. whimpering; whining
J - 9. REPLENISH		I. spirit; spunk
M - 10. NIMBLE		J. restock
P - 11. EFFICACY		K. dreadful; awful
Q - 12. DESOLATE		L. sympathy; caring
T - 13. RELUCTANT		M. lively; quick
H - 14. MEWLING		N. scolding
S - 15. SOLEMNITY		O. rich; fine
L - 16. COMPASSION		P. effectiveness; capability
B - 17. HEEDLESS		Q. deserted; abandoned
E - 18. STANCHING		R. opposition
K - 19. DIRE		S. seriousness
F - 20. TANTALIZINGLY		T. unwilling

VOCABULARY WORKSHEET 2 - *The Midwife's Apprentice*

____ 1. TREACHERY   A. sympathy; caring

____ 2. SUNDRY   B. opposition

____ 3. ABBEY   C. betrayal; disloyalty

____ 4. RESISTANCE   D. many; numerous

____ 5. ABUNDANCE   E. mocked; sneered

____ 6. HAGGLING   F. effectiveness; capability

____ 7. STOUT   G. plenty

____ 8. GLUTTONY   H. convent; monastery

____ 9. REVELERS   I. rambled

____ 10. STUPEFIED   J. drinkers; carousers

____ 11. COMPASSION   K. dishonor

____ 12. DECEIT   L. spirit; spunk

____ 13. HEEDLESS   M. heavy set

____ 14. PLUCK   N. excessive overeating

____ 15. RESOUNDED   O. an outhouse

____ 16. TAUNTED   P. dishonesty

____ 17. EFFICACY   Q. astonished; shocked

____ 18. DISREPUTE   R. unmindful

____ 19. MEANDERED   S. bartering; dickering

____ 20. PRIVY   T. echoed

KEY: VOCABULARY WORKSHEET 2 - *The Midwife's Apprentice*

C - 1. TREACHERY		A. sympathy; caring
D - 2. SUNDRY		B. opposition
H - 3. ABBEY		C. betrayal; disloyalty
B - 4. RESISTANCE		D. many; numerous
G - 5. ABUNDANCE		E. mocked; sneered
S - 6. HAGGLING		F. effectiveness; capability
M - 7. STOUT		G. plenty
N - 8. GLUTTONY		H. convent; monastery
J - 9. REVELERS		I. rambled
Q - 10. STUPEFIED		J. drinkers; carousers
A - 11. COMPASSION		K. dishonor
P - 12. DECEIT		L. spirit; spunk
R - 13. HEEDLESS		M. heavy set
L - 14. PLUCK		N. excessive overeating
T - 15. RESOUNDED		O. an outhouse
E - 16. TAUNTED		P. dishonesty
F - 17. EFFICACY		Q. astonished; shocked
K - 18. DISREPUTE		R. unmindful
I - 19. MEANDERED		S. bartering; dickering
O - 20. PRIVY		T. echoed

VOCABULARY JUGGLE LETTER REVIEW GAME CLUES - *The Midwife's Apprentice*

SCRAMBLED	WORD	CLUE
YAZAITNGILTNL	TANTALIZINGLY	fascinatingly
MGTENFENIR	FERMENTING	ripening
UXIUSRULO	LUXURIOUS	rich; fine
YTGNLTOU	GLUTTONY	excessive overeating
TREDICSHNE	CHRISTENED	named
ENSLLU	SULLEN	silent
UTTMHIARPN	TRIUMPHANT	victorious
SAEDOLET	DESOLATE	deserted; abandoned
NRCEIOAGN	IGNORANCE	unawareness; inexperience
BABYE	ABBEY	convent; monastery
GGLNIGHA	HAGGLING	bartering; dickering
INIOTNAVON	INNOVATION	an improvement
STHIO	HOIST	lift up
NCPECNEEITOM	INCOMPETENCE	stupidity; inability
PESDFTUEI	STUPEFIED	astonished; shocked
BLNEIM	NIMBLE	lively; quick
NWEGMLI	MEWLING	whimpering; whining
HRFHOETCEN	HENCEFORTH	from now on
MTEYIOSNL	SOLEMNITY	seriousness
RCVUSIOOTI	VICTORIOUS	successful
LTGIBH	BLIGHT	curse
SODDNEEUR	RESOUNDED	echoed
FILFBIA	BAILIFF	arresting officer
DMUIOCPMNE	COMPENDIUM	comprehensive summary
EHNSRPEIL	REPLENISH	restock
IDETEC	DECEIT	dishonesty
LEEVERSR	REVELERS	drinkers; carousers
UNSRYD	SUNDRY	many; numerous
ROUVSOIG	VIGOROUS	energetic
ONWNRDEE	RENOWNED	famous
OOSRSYHTAE	SOOTHSAYER	prophets; fortunetellers

www.ingramcontent.com/pod-product-compliance
Lightning Source LLC
Chambersburg PA
CBHW051410070526
44584CB00023B/3368